Beth Richards

Life

A VOLUME PACKED FULL OF PROSE & POETRY

Beth Richards

Life

A VOLUME PACKED FULL OF PROSE & POETRY

MEMOIRS

Cirencester

ALSO BY BETH RICHARDS

Reflections in Verse
ISBN: 0-7223 3578-4,
Arthur H Stockwell, 2005

Chill Out With Beth
Gems for Young and Old!
ISBN: 0-595-37203-1
iUniverse 2005

W O W: Words of Wisdom
ISBN: 0-595-40724-2
iUniverse 2006

Journey Towards a Dream
A Novel
ISBN: 0-595-42834-7
iUniverse 2007

Worlds Apart
Poems of Contrast
by Beth Richards & Charles Muller
ISBN: 0-595-50302-0
iUniverse 2008

Light Reading
Reflections from Poems and Prose
by Beth Richards
ISBN: 978-0-9559852-9-4
Diadem Books 2008

Darkness to Light
Further Enlightening Poetry and Prose
by Beth Richards
ISBN: 978-1907294075
Diadem Books 2009

Food for Thought
Savouring the Delights of Poetry & Prose
by Beth Richards
ISBN: 978-1907294440
Diadem Books 2010

Epic Times, Past and Present
Reflections in Prose and Poetry
by Beth Richards
ISBN: 978-1908026095
Diadem Books 2011

Pause for Thought
With Versastyle Poetry
by Beth Richards
ISBN: 978-1908026361
Diadem Books 2011

Turn the Page
A Volume of Short Stories
by Beth Richards
ISBN: 978-1908026502
Diadem Books 2012

Published by Memoirs

MEMOIRS
PUBLISHING

25 Market Place, Cirencester, Gloucestershire, GL7 2NX
info@memoirsbooks.co.uk www.memoirspublishing.com

ISBN: 978-1-909304-78-9

DEDICATION

My love as always goes to Geoff for supporting me all the way. Without his help there wouldn't be *Life*, my largest volume yet of Prose and Poetry.

Love you Geoff,

Topsy.X

ACKNOWLEDGEMENTS

Anyone who reads these stories, I would like them to soak up the atmosphere within them. Many of the poems, whether 'Free Verse' or Rhyming are based on imagination. I have experienced some of them first hand! I'll leave it to you, the reader, to deduce which constitute reality!

If readers place themselves in the part of the main character, this is exactly what I'm hoping for. Just like Shakespeare or Charles Dickens, my writing conveys living life as in the real world. Just as we travel through 'life' (the title of my book), so does 'The Tree of Life' (my cover oil painting) grow upwards, reaching towards the heavens.

Once again I thank my friends for confiding in me, thereby giving me ideas on which to write. I only hope that I've done justice to them!

Beth

II

FOREWORD

Beth has long enjoyed the reputation, in her writings, as a 'wise owl'. She has the perspicacity of seeing 'deep down things', right into the heart of things and has the ability to speak for many of us who are growing older, approaching retirement, and combining the wisdom of our years with the frustrations of age, when we become disillusioned with money spent on material gain instead of alleviating poverty, and become fed up with tailgaters driving too close to us! Well done, Beth - you are not afraid to speak out and provide a voice for us golden oldies who often suffer the indignity of being invisible to the younger generation who live at a different pace.

Most touching is Beth's evocation, on behalf of many of us, of memories and longings from days gone by - the longings for lost intimacies, of treasured moments no longer there, of being held and comforted; yet through her prose and poems we can share the re-evocation of such moments, even 'Reliving that tingling sensation before the explosion'! Her writings highlight the value of such memories, but especially the value of enduring friendships, even if some of these are sacred friendships hidden in the depths of the heart and secret thoughts. Beth has the soul of a poet and she is not afraid to bare her soul, however sensitive, and it's this sincere and honest quality that will make the reader feel like a close friend.

Charles Muller
MA (Wales), PhD (Lond), MEd, DEd (SA), DLitt (UOFS)

PREFACE

Life is just that! It's all about our journey through life. Beginning with birth, travelling towards an inevitable demise! The ups and downs of coping with all eventualities!

First of all, the story 'Love Divine' is inspired by a question! 'Do you believe in love at first sight?' This story is an account of how my parents met and married! I penned this on behalf of Phoebe, my mother, who went blind when she was only 71 years of age - caused by neglect and Glaucoma (a serious eye disease).

The second part is an autobiography of my life, from birth to the present day (retirement).

Finally, the biography of my daughter and her life. All in all, the story of three generations.

As we journey through life, we encounter many people who become friends… others are merely acquaintances. If we're fortunate we make a few lifetime friends! I am fortunate and have a few very dear friends.

'Retirement'… well, that's another story, in which I've tried to convey that 'life isn't always greener…' It has some disadvantages as well as advantages! Whatever anyone does when they reach retirement is entirely up to the individual.

Many people long to travel, go on a cruise… things they couldn't afford to do in their working life. Maybe, for the first time in their life, they have both, the money and time to pursue their dream.

Many people long for retirement with the idea that they can take life at a slower pace. That old proverb 'I don't know how I found time to go to work' is so correct, but we can't understand this when we're young. It's not until you reach retirement age that you realise just how quickly time flies. For one thing, the simple tasks take so much longer to perform as you grow older.

For myself, I get very angry at times. This occurs because I have a very active mind and when my body refuses to co-operate it frustrates me greatly. Thankfully, writing has become my saviour! As well as writing, I also paint in oils. I took this up as another hobby when I retired and I make a point of designing and painting the cover of my books! The painting on the cover is again one that I've painted especially for this latest volume of poetry and prose and is entitled: 'The Tree of Life.'

Retirement gave me time. In other words, 'me'-time to pursue hobbies that I'd not had time for when I was younger. I get absorbed in painting since it's a great way of relaxing and opting out of other problems. When I write, whether it's poetry or prose, I'm really painting a picture in WORDS. Many people read and visit a world of imagination, which is what I hope you'll do now... read *Life*... escape and enjoy!

Beth Richards

PAUSE AND GIVE THOUGHT

Everything we do in life begins with 'an idea'. Everyone has a dream. Many of us have a fear of something. The secret of success is how we deal with everything.

Do you face up to your fears, or run away?

Do you always 'practice what you preach'?

So many questions. So many answers.

The pattern of life is full of obstacles. Are you a pessimist, or an optimist?

Are you a half empty glass, or a half full glass person?

Everything happens for a reason, we're told.

My theory for this is: Look for the silver lining, there always is one… find it!

This is something we're all guilty of… when we're in trouble - we pray to God for help.

Our prayers aren't always answered as we'd like. I believe this is what is meant when it is said that 'everything happens for a reason!'

Finally, because everything we do begins with 'an idea' and every one of us has a dream… do as the philosopher wrote:

> Whatever you can do, or dream you can, begin it.
> Boldness has genius, power and magic in it,
> Begin it now…

Just as I have tried to do once again.

Beth Richards

TABLE OF CONTENTS

TABLE OF CONTENTS

PROSE

LOVE DIVINE

PART ONE: PHOEBE

⌒

I'd been working at the George and Dragon for ten years. Little did I know that very night I would meet my future husband, Frank, and fall head over heels in love.

It truly was 'love at first sight' - after all, I'd been courting the landlord's son for nine of these years, and still I was a spinster!

All this happened years ago now. This is my story.

*　*　*

My name is Phoebe. Without looking obvious I espied a newcomer that night in the George and Dragon. He sat alone, and after three nights I was intrigued. Somehow he looked out of place... and the following night I made a point of serving him. He was softly spoken and I could tell he wasn't from around these parts. That night he came back for another drink and asked, 'Eh lass, can I be so bold as to walk you home when you finish?' I liked the sound of his voice and accepted his offer. Little did he know just how far it was to 'home'!

He told me his name was Frank, and he met me later that night when I finished behind the bar. He was quite tall with jet black hair and a broad frame. What some might call, 'tall, dark and handsome!'

As we walked along he told me a bit about himself, how he'd cycled down from the north in search of work. He'd lost his cattle and farm, he was penniless... maybe I felt sorry for him at first, but in my heart I knew we were somehow destined to be together.

By this time he'd placed his arm around my shoulder... it felt comfortable. It didn't enter my head that he was being forward in doing so. At one point Frank did ask, 'How much further lass?'

'Only round the corner,' I replied.

A little further on and he said, 'How many more corners then?'

'Nearly there,' I replied!

Eventually we reached my parents' cottage where he bade me goodnight in a gentlemanly fashion.

Cheekily he called out to me: 'I'll see you again Phoebe, same time, same place - The George and Dragon.'

That night, lying in my bed, I knew that my courtship with John was over. I simply didn't feel the same towards him now that Frank had entered my life. I realised now that John had always been the brother I'd never had the joy of sharing my life with.

Pity my parents didn't understand me in all this. But that's another part of my story.

*   *   *

Every night Frank turned up at the George and Dragon. Gradually I got to know and understand him... and why he'd come south. Just two months later he asked me to marry him and without any hesitation I answered, 'Yes!'

Now things were serious, it was time to take Frank home to meet my parents. In my mind I knew they weren't going to be in raptures about our engagement, but I had to introduce them to my husband to be. I didn't expect quite such an outrage though!

My parents were very Victorian in their outlook, so I shouldn't have been so surprised. You see, John was so different to Frank. John was in a good position with him being the Landlord's son at the George and Dragon... whereas Frank was penniless, or very nearly. Also, I'd been going out with John for nine years, whereas I'd only known Frank for a couple of months! My parents thought I must be mad. We were in the front parlour and father shouted at me, 'If you marry this man, you'll never darken these doors again!'

The choice wasn't a hard one to make. 'Come on Frank, we're leaving'... and that was that. Before we left, though, I said to my father, 'I'm 35 years old, I know what I'm doing, I'm not listening to you this time.' And with that said, we left. I felt sad for my mother, but for once in my life I knew that I was right. I loved Frank too much to change my mind.

Exactly one month later Frank and I married at the local

registry office, with just two witnesses from off the street. I was now Mrs Richardson. This was exactly three months after Frank and I met.

In the meantime Frank had secured a gardener's job, with a tied cottage. (Not the best of arrangements, but beggars can't be choosers.) At least we had somewhere to live.

During the first eighteen months of our marriage we had many moves.

My mother and I agreed to let bygones be bygones, and eventually my father came round to accepting that I was now married and I began to visit them again... on my own at the beginning.

One morning I received a letter. Opening it, I realised it was from John. It began: 'Dear Em...' It was only John who'd ever called me Em. (My second name being Emily.) He said he would be pleased to see me again and wished me well as he'd heard that I was now married to Frank.

I said nothing about this to Frank, and the next time I visited my parents I arranged to go and see John at the George and Dragon.

It seemed surreal walking down the road again, retracing steps I'd walked for so many years. It was showery; raindrops glistened on the carpeted green... It was a Sunday morning and the church bells rang out as I walked along. For some reason I felt nervous; maybe it was because I hadn't mentioned to Frank where I was going - besides visiting my parents. Was it guilt that I felt?

John greeted me, pressing his cheek to mine, then leaned back, studying me closely. 'You're looking well Em,' he said. 'Married life suits you. Come on into the back, you know your way.'

The small back room was more private. It was then John drew me into his arms, planting a kiss on my lips. I was surprised to say the least. Although John and I had been courting for nine years, he'd never been very demonstrative... and me a married woman now!

'I've never forgotten you, you know. I wanted to see you and make sure that you're happy, Em,'he said. He mentioned hearing tales about my parents not being pleased with my marriage to Frank.

'That's an understatement,' I added. To change the subject I asked him how his father was?

'Getting older Em, and he always thought that you'd be his daughter-in-law one day.' He looked sad as he said this. 'I always thought you'd marry me too.'

We sat having a drink, talking about old times before I left. John gave me a quick peck on the cheek before he waved me off into the dusk. That was the last time I saw John. He didn't contact me again: he must have been satisfied that I was happy.

A few months after Frank and I married, Joe and Jeanie moved down from the north. This was Frank's younger brother. They'd always been very close, so Frank helped instigate this. They'd departed in some degree of haste.

Jeanie was a married woman, and in those days for a man to have an affair with a married woman was very scandalous behaviour. But one doesn't always choose wisely when one falls in love. Frank helped them to find work and somewhere to live. In addition to this, their house was large enough for them to take in a couple of lodgers to swell the funds!

Frank and Joe's father came down to visit Joe and see their new home. He liked it so much that he never returned to the north and stayed with Joe and Jeanie until he died. He was widowed early in life. Frank was only seventeen when his mother died. She'd given birth to ten children, Frank being the eldest. She'd had a hard life, and women didn't live to an old age in those days.

Frank and I had been married for eight months when, shock horror... I found out I was pregnant! Because I was well into my thirties I was quite alarmed at the thought of having a baby. In those days having a baby at such a late age was almost like having a death sentence imposed on one. I was afraid, and other women didn't help by telling me horrendous tales of their childbirth experiences.

Georgina was born on the 5th August at 4.10 a.m., and I spent my 37th birthday in bed with her. Just ten days later I was up and walking down the garden path. I'd survived, although Georgie (as we called her) was quite a large baby, weighing in at 9lb.4oz! Frank had wanted a son and we'd chosen to call him George... hence when our daughter was born, it seemed appropriate to name her Georgina.

This was in 1937 and war was looming on the horizon. What a world to bring a baby into! Because of the war, Georgie was our only daughter. Frank and I moved from Marlow, Bucks to Windsor where Frank got a job as a stonemason on Windsor Castle.

Georgie was two years old when we moved to Windsor. When she started school she was a sickly child and caught every ailment that children get. Because of this I may have been over protective of her. We lived in a flat, three stories high… in the town centre and because of this she couldn't go out to play. She was a lonely, only child.

In 1939 war was declared, the war to end all wars we were told. We were led to believe very optimistically that the war would be over by Christmas, but it went on for six long years.

Georgie was only two years old when war was declared. This robbed her, together with many thousands of children, of their safe childhood. She didn't visit the seaside until she was nine years old, when the beaches had been cleared of mines etc., and were safe.

Georgie was the apple of Frank's eye, and I often felt jealous. Yes, jealous of my own daughter! Frank was very musical: he'd belonged to a brass band up north in Alstonefield, his own village where he was born and he joined the Marlow town band after he came south. I wasn't musical, but his brother Joe got a piano for Georgie and Frank paid for her to have piano lessons. She took to it like a duck to water! I suppose, because of where we lived and the fact that she couldn't go out to play, she practised for hours. (It drove me crazy at times!) However, Frank encouraged her, standing beside her and making sure she kept in time. (It really was music to Frank's ears.)

Georgie was her teacher's star pupil, passing exams at speed with honours and distinction. By the time she was twelve she was ready to apply for a place at college, and would have obtained a grant to help pay for this. The college was in Reading, Berkshire, eighteen miles away. I couldn't agree to her going away from home, although it caused arguments between Frank and me. I got my own way and she didn't go! I don't think she forgave me for a long time, if ever. Although Georgie continued playing her piano as well as the piano and organ at our Methodist chapel, I think she lost a lot of her enthusiasm. She'd wanted to become a concert pianist, and this wasn't going to happen after I'd refused to let her go to college.

When Georgie was sixteen, her uncle Joe was diagnosed with lung cancer! He'd always been a heavy drinker and smoker, but so had my father and he was much older than Joe, and still going strong. Why did this have to happen to Joe? When Joe entered hospital for an operation they found that he'd always had a weak heart. (No one knew this.) He lived for just six months. Frank was devastated when Joe died. Frank and I went to the funeral, but thought it best if Georgie didn't. We did this for the best of reasons: she was Joe's favourite niece, and we knew she'd be engulfed in grief.

With hindsight, I don't think we did right, for Georgie never got to say goodbye to her uncle and I think she resented us again.

Georgie was always a wilful child, and things seemed to be getting worse. She brought a few boyfriends home, mostly ones we didn't approve of. Then she met Brian through her work and once again we didn't like her choice... but this time she stood her ground. She must have really loved Brian: it didn't matter what we said, she took no notice.

In the meantime Jeanie wanted to return north. We tried to persuade her to stay where she and Joe had been happy. She wasn't on her own as she had a couple of lodgers and her job. We went to see her and try to talk some sense into her. While we were driving along she suddenly opened the car door and jumped out to her death! She'd threatened to do it just before she opened the car door... but we thought she was bluffing! Again, we were wrong.

Georgie shouted at us when we arrived home and told her what had happened. 'Why do you always think you know best!' she cried out.

Soon after her outburst, she told us that she and Brian were getting married at the local registry office in Windsor. We tried to get them to change their minds and have a quiet church wedding, but she was adamant. 'It was good enough for you, and it's good enough for us,' she said.

We were getting too old to argue now, so a registry office wedding was what they had. It seemed that history had repeated itself in so far as my parents had been against Frank and me getting married. Although Georgie knew we were against her marrying Brian, she was strong willed and defied us. (Just as I had defied my parents!) I can only hope they'll be happy together, that Georgie won't have regrets. Because all appears 'hunky dory' to the onlooker, our marriage hasn't all been a bed of roses… We only remained together because of Georgie!

Georgie was different to me. Once they got established with a home she desperately wanted a baby. Each month she got frustrated when her period arrived.

Although it meant catching two buses I went and saw Georgie quite often. She told me that she'd always wanted 'a husband, house and baby - in that order.' She'd got Brian and a house, but as yet, no baby!

Georgie took a part-time job in the afternoons. Her doctor had advised her to stop thinking about having a baby so much… and then it would probably happen. She even had tests at the hospital, but they didn't show any abnormality. At the time I remember saying to her, 'I admire you young people going to work to get things for your home.' BUT, the real reason for Georgie going out in the afternoons was to take her mind off her longing for a baby. It took Georgie and Brian four long years before she at last became pregnant. But that's another story!

I really couldn't understand how Georgie could want a baby so desperately. She really didn't know what she was in for… Also, how life is never the same once you have a child.

A neighbour asked me one day, 'Is Georgie happy?' I replied, 'Well, she should be; she has a house and a car, why shouldn't she be happy?'

Frank came from the north where they treat their women differently. I never enjoyed the physical side of marriage, and to be honest when we married I didn't contemplate having a child or children, whereas Frank said he wouldn't have got married if he thought we would be childless. As the years rolled by Frank became more demanding; whether I wanted sex or not, he would force the issue for his own gratification. They say 'Hate and love are much akin' - how true that can be.

I had been ill for some time, and Frank did his best to look after me in his own rough fashion. I was in bed, unable to raise my head when I had an accident when vomiting... and he suddenly raised his arms and began punching me, vile language spilling forth as he did so. All went black as I passed out and the next I knew, I came to in hospital with a broken leg and ribs!

As soon as she knew, Georgie came to see me and wanted to know the truth. 'Whatever happened, mum?' I never did tell her. I was loyal to Frank. Gradually those wonderful nurses and doctors mended my broken bones, but inside I still hurt at what Frank had done to me. When one marries, (even in a registry office), one makes vows to care for each other 'in sickness and in health, until death do us part'. In my mind Frank had let me down.

It took a long time for my bones to heal before I was sent

for convalescence. When the time was right, I was taken home to see how I'd cope... I made sure I didn't do well, and at a later date I went into a care home. No way could I face living with Frank again after what he'd done to me!

Georgie, bless her, came to visit me every Saturday morning. We'd had our differences in the past, but she didn't let me down when I needed her.

I loved her, BUT I could see that in the past I'd smothered her, not mothered her. I had hours to sit and think about the past, but we only get one shot at life and we're none of us perfect. I'd made mistakes, which I regretted, but there was nothing I could do about it.

I remember asking Georgie once, 'Please don't desert me.' She never did.

To enable me to write this story I had to enlist the help of Georgie, the reason being I am now blind. I SO wanted to write this story to show how coincidences occur often in a lifetime. After all, if Frank had never entered my life, would I have eventually settled down with John? Even I don't know the answer to that.

PART TWO: GEORGIE

Part One of 'Love Divine' I wrote on behalf of my mother, Pheobe. I would like you to read Part Two now, written by myself, Georgie.

History repeated itself as you will find later on in my story.

Also coincidences occur so often, it's unbelievable at times.

This, then is MY story of MY life... with its incredible ups and downs! I really didn't want to end up like my mother, but however hard we try not to... inevitably we do become like our mothers. In our later years, and this is true in my case, we find ourselves uttering the same words as our mothers.

* * *

My life began on the 5th August 1937 at 4.10 a.m., so my mother told me. I was there, but of course I don't remember it. I weighed in at 9lb.4oz, a healthy weight. To begin with, my mother, Phoebe, and I belong to the same star sign - Leo! Leo's can be possessive, over protective; just as a lioness is with her cubs, my mother was with me. This isn't mother love, it's smother love.

I only know this fact (about me being a mistake) because my father told me. Phoebe, my mother, told everyone that I was a mistake... only to be corrected by my father who interrupted her one day, saying, 'I wouldn't have got married if I hadn't thought we'd have a child.'

In the first two years of my life my parents moved many times. That was until war broke out and they moved to a flat in Windsor, Berkshire. Because this flat was three storeys high above a shop in the main street, I was unable to go out to play. It wouldn't have been safe with traffic and buses, etc. So I was a very lonely, only child. I wasn't lucky enough to have any siblings; with war looming on the horizon my parents decided it wasn't a very nice world for another baby to be born into. Anyway, I don't think my mother was very maternal! After all, it seemed that she didn't really want me in the first place!

I don't know what age a child remembers from; for me it was around the age of four. I was only two years old when World War II broke out in 1939. The war to end all wars, everyone was told... but it lasted for six years. I do remember vividly the bombing raids at night, the sirens blaring during daytime, people rushing down to air raid shelters. Windsor was a Garrison town, soldiers regularly seen in the streets, day and night.

During the war years food was in short supply with ration books… no sweets, not much fruit, and children had very few toys. Children were robbed of so many things during this period. Many were evacuated away to the country for their own safety. Some never saw their parents again... Even if they did, it could be many years later. Life was hard, but we Brits are known for stamina and courage... pulling together in times of need!

It was 1945 when the war finally ended. I was eight years old by then. I was nine years old when I saw the sea for the first time. Until then the beaches weren't safe, for mines had to be cleared from them.

I was a sickly child and caught almost everything going. My mother used to delight in telling everyone what a sickly child I was! I caught scarlet fever, and the doctor wanted me to be admitted to hospital, but Mother fought to keep me at home. This wasn't easy; for one thing she had no washing machine... they hadn't been invented in those days. She had to wash, dry and iron in that dreadful flat with no proper sanitation. It's a wonder I survived! I vividly remember her borrowing a pushchair to take me out and get some fresh air....I was very weak after the scarlet fever. Although I don't think she wanted a child, she enjoyed having me at home when I was sick, so at the least sign of a temperature, the thermometer was popped into my mouth and I was kept indoors that day.

Like most children I didn't always do as I was told. My mother got so angry at times, she would thrash me and scream at me: 'If you don't do as I tell you, I'll break every bone in your body!' She frightened me so much. I don't remember my father ever laying a hand on me. I really envy children who can say they had a happy childhood. I certainly didn't.

*   *   *

I remember my first day at school. I was five years old and it was the first time I'd been separated from my mother. I didn't like school much... and things didn't improve over the years. I hated it and couldn't wait to leave. Ten whole years of going to school, unhappy and uninterested... I couldn't see the point of learning about Henry VIII and his wives, etc. It was boring. Because of this, when I did leave, I had no qualifications whatsoever. Luckily I had very good handwriting. Whenever I applied for a job I almost certainly got an interview... even, if not the job!

Phoebe, my mother, wanted me to be a dressmaker, and I wanted to be a hairdresser! Neither of us won that battle, because I became a secretary. When I was a child she ill-treated me, and we were still clashing when I grew up. She would shout at me saying, 'After all I sacrificed for you, and this is how you treat me!' How can a mother say that to her child? Every mother makes sacrifices for her child. After all, children don't ask to be born!

I had many different jobs to begin with before I eventually settled down. Maybe this difficulty in finding employment was down to the fact that in my heart I'd wanted to be a concert pianist. My uncle Joe had bought me a piano, and my father paid for me to have piano lessons and this was what I wanted out of life. By the age of twelve I was ready for college, having passed exams with honours and distinction. BUT, Phoebe, my dear mother refused to let me go, although my teacher assured my parents that I was so good I would have gained a grant towards the cost. My mother wasn't musical like my father, who'd played instruments in a brass band. (She had such a hold over my father that she wasn't happy until he gave up playing in the band.) She couldn't understand my dream of becoming a concert pianist, and my father was too weak willed to go against her!

After that I still played and accompanied singers at our Methodist Church, but the enthusiasm, my dreams of becoming a concert pianist were dashed. Gradually over the years I played less and less. I don't think I ever really forgave my mother for refusing to let me go to college!

*   *   *

My first long term job was in a builders office, as the office junior. (Tea making, doing the post at night, etc., and learning the ropes.) It was there I was attracted to Harry, my boss, a married man with a wife and two children. He, who should have known better, made advances to me and I was too naïve to resist him. I really thought I loved him - how stupid I was. But everything is easy with hindsight, and I should have known better than to think I was anything more than his 'bit on the side'. I stayed there for eighteen months, then applied for a job with another local builder. I was heartbroken when I left. All Harry said was, 'I shall miss you,' and that was that.

The first few weeks in my new job were not good. I was totally miserable. I walked my dog past Harry's house, in the hopes of seeing him... but I never did. Alone in my room at home, I played my favourite records, mostly love ballads. To say I was depressed, very distressed, would be an understatement.

I managed to make friends with a couple of girls I got

talking to in the local sandwich bar. This helped, but was no substitute for my longing to see Harry. Silly me...

My new boss was old enough to be my grandfather. He smoked large Havana cigars which filled my small office with fumes. Sometimes this was bad enough to send for the fire brigade. He also drank heavily at the Criterion PH. Those fumes were enough to intoxicate me. At least, there was no chance of my falling in love again with the boss. But he thought the world of me and we got on well together.

What I hadn't bargained for was the young man who worked in the shop next door. His name was Brian, and for some reason he liked what he saw when I stood in the shop window that adjoined my office. Funnily enough, both Brian and his apprentice came round one afternoon to borrow 'Big Bertha' (the builders' term for a very large ladder) and I stood talking to the pair of them... but it was Tom I fancied and flirted with - not knowing that he was newly married. Oh dear....

That evening while walking my dog Brian came screeching to a halt on his old bike right beside me. He asked me outright, 'What are you doing later?'

'Not a lot,' I replied.

'Well, how about meeting me about 7 p.m. and we'll go for a walk?' he said.

Last of the big spenders, I thought to myself, but I agreed to go for a walk with him. Brian then sped off on his old push bike while I took Ben, my dog, home.

Brian and I walked along the tow path of the river Thames. It was getting chilly and Brian put his arm around my shoulder. It was early April, and it's often cold near water... Also, the moonlight gave me the idea that we could even get a slight frost. I shivered at the thought. Brian must have felt me shiver; he gripped my shoulder a little harder as though he knew what I was thinking.

We walked home, and before we parted he kissed me goodnight. I thought to myself, 'Cheeky monkey.'

'How about coming to the cinema tomorrow night?' he asked?

'Okay,' I answered, not very enthusiastically, but I had nothing better to do and that was why I agreed. That was to be the start of our courtship. Although I didn't know it just then, I'd met my future husband.

Before Brian came on the scene I'd had one other serious boyfriend... but Phoebe interfered and that was the end of that boyfriend. However, when I took Brian home, she was back to her old tricks again, only this time I was having none of it. They even forbade me to see him at one stage, but I defied them and threatened to leave home.

I'd grown up now, and came to the conclusion that Prince Charles himself wouldn't be accepted by my mother as a future son-in-law! I came to realise that Phoebe was thinking selfishly, and that I should stay single in order to look after her in her old age.

On the other hand, my father got on well with Brian...

but when it came to standing up to my mother he was weak willed.

The outcome was that Brian proposed to me just three months after we'd met, and I accepted. This did not stop Mother's intervention though. She was clever enough to vent her wrath on me when we were alone. Consequently, my father never heard her.

Brian and I got engaged FORMALLY exactly one year after we met. He was called up to do two years National Service one year later. We'd planned to wait until he came out of the Army, but being parted was very painful and in the May of 1957 we got married, after a two-year courtship.

Because Brian was being posted to Germany, I arranged our wedding with a special licence at the local Registry Office. It was a very quiet wedding. Once again Mother interfered - she wanted us to have a quiet church wedding. Neither Brian nor I wanted any fuss, so I stuck to my guns for the ceremony to be in the local Registry Office. Mother had never wanted me to marry Brian, and because I was under the age of 21, I had to get my parents' consent. Although she did sign the form of consent, she held the threat over me that she could withdraw it at any time. I remember very vividly standing in the Registry Office, when suddenly the thought came into mind that she could still stop us, and my leg suddenly shook at these thoughts! I remember the few in attendance thought I was going to collapse... but I didn't! Mother was friendly with the local vicar, and I never knew what he said to her; whatever it was had caused her to sign that consent form. (Thank the Lord!)

Someone said to me, 'I wouldn't feel married if it wasn't in a church.' I replied, 'God will bless our marriage wherever it takes place.' I took my marriage vows very seriously... they were not just words to me. I meant them with all my heart and soul.

Just ten days after our marriage Brian was posted to Germany and I didn't see him again for eight months. For the rest of his time in the army, I just existed... for part of me went with him to Germany. It was a very long two years for both of us. We were soul mates!

*   *   *

While Brian was away I continued to live with my parents. Since Brian and I had been together, all I'd wanted was a husband, house and baby, in that order. Well, I'd got the husband, so I'd made a start. However, we began married life in a mobile static caravan, with no running water or electricity. But, we were so happy being together again.

I vividly remember the morning mother waved me off for the final time. Me, lugging a very large suitcase and thinking to myself, 'At last I'm free!' I'd wanted freedom for such a long time. This was it! I felt liberated, like a caged animal set free. That same dark, snowy night (it was mid-January), I saw Brian coming up the path with his suitcase.

'This is it,' I thought, 'this is where our lives begin!' I thanked God that Brian had come back safely. Some of the boy's who'd been sent to Cyprus weren't so lucky. It wasn't war time, BUT Cyprus was well known for what they called 'Murder Mile' at that time.

With Brian away I'd sorted out our caravan home, with the help of Brian's cousin. My father told me, 'You don't have to do this, you can stay with us for a while.' What he didn't know was just how Mother tormented me, always in his absence!

It had been a kind of mental torture some times. Brian wrote to me daily, apart from when he was on manoeuvres; then I could receive two or three letters from a field post box. Mother would prop my letters on the sideboard where I could see them as soon as I entered the back door. I was always happy to see a letter. Sometimes, though, she would put the letter inside the drawer... then bring it out later. It was her idea of a joke! To me, though, I was like Queen Victoria when she said, 'We are not amused!'

Once home and Brian had to find a job, I was still working at the builders where I'd met Brian. Within a couple of weeks Brian started work as an electrician with a small firm in Eton. We now had two incomes to live on. Things were looking up!

Although our caravan was home to us, we didn't intend staying there any longer than we needed to. With this in mind, I scoured the local paper and applied for a job with the Windsor Group Hospital Management Committee, and was successful. I did this for one reason alone - the salary was good. Bill, my old boss, told me that he'd given me a good reference, saying that 'his loss was their gain'. I have to admit I was curious and wondered if he really had said this. One day I had to be in the office where all the files were kept and I took a chance, (there were other workers around), but I quickly found my file.... yes, Bill really had put those words on his reference to my new employers! I felt humbled to think that he thought so much of me. I hadn't realized this before.

After saving hard for six months, Brian and I had enough money for a deposit on a maisonette we'd seen and liked. We were granted a mortgage and this was the first step on the ladder to becoming property owners. (My father said we were mad, and would never get our money back.) However, we proved him wrong, and just twenty months later we sold the maisonette at a profit and put that money down on a semi-detached two bedroom house about a mile away. This was our home for the next 34 years!

I'd achieved two of my ambitions... my husband Brian, and a house! Unlike my mother, all I wanted now, was a baby. This proved very frustrating - each monthly bleed was agony to me. But as with everything in life, 'if you want something badly enough, you succeed' - and eventually I gave birth to baby Shirley. I now felt fulfilled in my new role as a mother. I'd found my niche in life.

Brian and I worked very hard to make our house into a home. We got on really well with our neighbours... a bit too well with one of them who told me one day that he was 'getting too fond of me'. This proved awkward.

Brian's brother called in often, especially if he had any problems. (He lived nearby.) I'd always got on well with him. On one such morning he'd called in for a coffee and confessed that he'd always fancied me, although he said I was no oil painting. I had suspected this for a long time. He'd been very good to us; he worked at a builders' merchants and regularly got us a discount on materials we needed for repairs to our home. Oh dear, this could prove difficult.

Brian had told me many times that I had 'sex appeal'... whatever that was! I'd been told by more than one man 'I had come to bed eyes'... whatever *that* was! Certainly I'd never intentionally given this impression to any man. Maybe it was my blonde hair that was the attraction. I couldn't change that, it was natural blonde.

I made plenty of friends, some with children. We'd meet at each other's houses and have a chat, cups of tea, while the children played. They were very happy days. I would walk for miles with Shirley in her pram. I found that everyone talks to you if you have either a baby or a dog.

Phoebe, my mother, would come over on the bus quite often. She would call in at the local M&S in town and buy some chocolate cakes for a treat. I didn't have much money in those days for luxuries.

Brian was allowed to bring his van home from his place of work, providing we had somewhere to park it off the road... which we had. I began to think that our car was standing idle in our garage most of the week for it only got used at the weekends. It would be handy if I could go shopping in the car instead of struggling with the pushchair onto a bus, with Shirley tucked under my arm. Sometimes if I was lucky, someone would help... but often as not I struggled. Also, it would prove helpful for me to take over some of the driving when we went on holiday.

I thought about this and suggested I learn to drive. Brian thought it a good idea, so I booked myself some driving lessons with a local school of motoring that taught on a mini. I was in my early thirties now and Shirley had begun school.

*   *   *

I was a complete novice, but it was nice to have another interest and I began to enjoy driving after the initial mistakes I made in the beginning. A friend advised me to wear trousers when I went for a lesson. That was good advice for my instructor had the habit of touching my knee - accidentally, on purpose I thought, when changing gear. Was I right?

My main problem was 'corners'. My instructor said, 'If you could go up to a corner in reverse you'd be okay.' He said this because reversing around corners and three point turns were a piece of cake to me. It was those blessed corners. I either approached them too slow, or too fast! Oh dear, when I'd watched Brian driving, it all looked so easy. (I really hadn't bargained for what I termed 'making it sit up and beg'.)

I chose to take my driving test locally. My instructor had great confidence that I would pass first time. However, I made one stupid mistake and failed. This didn't deter me though. I applied for a cancellation and just one month (and one lesson) later, I passed. Now, I could drive on my own, BUT... this is when one really begins to learn. When Brian came home for his lunchtime break, he said, 'Go on, take the car for a quick drive locally; you know you have to go on your own sometime and the longer you leave it the worse you'll feel.' With nervous apprehension I took the keys, backed off the driveway and away I went. I planned my route, and with caution, kept to left-hand turnings where possible. It didn't take me long, but when I arrived back home, (car still intact)... I felt triumphant. After a few trips out on my own I began to wonder why I'd made such a fuss about driving. It was a piece of cake. I now had the freedom of the road, to come and go as I pleased.

I was, however, a very cautious driver, and when I took a neighbour shopping he would say, 'Go on, you have the right of way'....to which I replied, 'Yes, I do have the right of way, but I don't want to dent the car.'

Brian gradually climbed the ladder at his work and

became a Foreman, then finally a Sales Rep., which included a company car, a good perk of the job at the time. Things were looking up for us. We afforded a two-week summer holiday, which we often took down in the South Hams, a beautiful part of Devon near Kingsbridge.

After one of our two week breaks in Devon, we arrived home and I went round to see Jeff and Frances, our neighbours. Only Jeff was in and he greeted me warmly. I stupidly asked, 'Have you missed me?' To my utter surprise he said 'YES' and kissed me full on the lips! I had no idea he would do such a thing.

Maybe Jeff felt something for me because he was a very keen gardener. Often on a summer's evening he would be out in his garden, which ran across the bottom of our garden and we would discuss many things, some of them quite personal. However this made things a little awkward. I was friends with Frances and tried to make sure that Jeff wasn't on his own when I went round. He had a grown up son and I certainly didn't feel anything towards Jeff. (Not in that way!)

One Christmas Brian and I went round for a drink. Jeff was quite insistent that I try some 'Southern Comfort'. He was convinced I would love it. I didn't. That didn't go down well with Jeff.

At Christmas time Brian and I had our log fire going. It was the one time of year we used it. We loved it - there's nothing like logs crackling and hissing, and flames spiralling up the chimney, with a glass of sherry and some mince pies to hand. We always invited our other neighbours, Don and Hazel, round on Boxing morning for a drink and homemade mince pies. Although Hazel didn't like the mess of a coal and log fire, she admitted there was nothing like the real fire. They would come to us one year and we'd go to them the following year. They were happy days.

Another friend of ours was Den, and I always visited him on Christmas morning. He was a widower living on his own and hated Christmas. He had just one son living at home. Whilst I was in his kitchen one year, Carl, a neighbour of his, called (as I had done) to see if he was okay. Carl knocked on Den's back door. He towered above me... and swept me in his arms, gave me a whopping kiss and wished me a 'Happy Christmas'. Again, that was a total surprise... but a nice one!

Besides our fortnight in Devon in the summer, we'd drive down to Hayling Island sometimes just for a day at the weekend. Shirley loved the sea, and so did Pickles our dog. He was a funny little dog. At home he would walk around any puddles, as though he didn't like getting his feet wet... but as soon as we approached the sea, his nose would go up as he sniffed the ozone. He loved paddling in the sea. Dogs aren't stupid. He was full of rheumatism and the salt water was good for this.

* * *

Brian talked me into buying a touring caravan, and at the age of 40 we trekked up the M1 Motorway to meet an uncle and aunt of mine for the first time. I'd never seen such beautiful scenery in my life... not even in Devon. I was smitten, and couldn't get enough of it.

I got to know my five cousins. I got very fond of Robert, who became like a brother to me. We both loved music, and Robert had a wonderful studio with his equipment set up. I'd go out with him and we'd enjoy the music and just sit talking, enjoying the atmosphere. Rob was divorced, but still loved his ex-wife, who'd gone off with another man and had a child by him. He was easy to talk with and yes, I did become very fond of him and during the months when we didn't visit... I'd sit and think of Rob, looking forward to being with him again, especially on a Saturday night, listening to music together.

We'd become close; he'd confide in me, telling me things I don't think he'd told many others about. I couldn't understand how Margaret could leave Rob. He had a beard, very unruly curly black hair and was a very attractive bloke. It made me feel sad that inwardly he was hurting. We'd definitely bonded... the feelings we had were mutual.

During this period of my life I began writing poetry. The very first piece I ever wrote was on a winter's afternoon and it was snowing heavily in Windsor. It was unusual for snow to fall in Berkshire. Brian sent my poem to his magazine where he worked and they printed it... I didn't get any payment, but it was a thrilling moment seeing something I'd written in print! It was entitled 'Snowflakes':

The snow falls gently,
falling in from outer space;
The flakes are all so different,
but each one is full of grace.
It settles down in silence,
on the hillsides all around;
It wraps us like a blanket,
as it covers up the ground.
Spring will come quite suddenly,
the warm air brings a thaw;
Our pretty snowflakes vanish,
into outer space once more.

After writing this I was hooked on writing poetry. If I was sad, it comforted me... I could write down my feelings if anyone hurt me. It was something akin to therapy. (I wasn't aware of this at that time, but later on in life I began writing poetry as a hobby in retirement.) This will be mentioned at the end of my story.

Uncle Peter and Aunt Gina always welcomed us very cordially. They had a stone built farmhouse with oak beams. Uncle had now given up raising cattle and rented out many acres of his land. Saturday nights sitting in their front room, a blazing fire roaring in the stone fireplace, was warm and intimate. Pickles loved the fire, occasionally jumping when the log spat… but it didn't deter him.

Uncle would sit by the Aga in the kitchen and have his supper. One such Saturday night he placed his beef sandwich down beside him and Pickles somehow stole it. Uncle loved dogs, which was good because he never scolded Pickles for stealing his supper. In fact, it was a joke that was told over and over again… how Pickles ate his sandwich!

One winter's afternoon I was at home and I felt depressed. I sat longing to see Rob, the poetry began to flow and I wrote a piece, entitled 'Dream Cottage.' It came to me easily as I'd confided in Rob, one Saturday night, how I'd love to retire one day to Derbyshire. At that stage in my life it was a dream… but dreams do sometimes come true if you want them badly enough. (And I wanted it badly.)

'Dream Cottage'

Cottages, log fires,
and old oak beams,
are they a possibility,
a reality,
or are they like a lot of things,
just dreams?
Only time can give the answer,
be it yes or no.

Do we stay as we are,
or do we have a go?
The answer lies within ourselves,
the choice is ours to make,
do we go on as we are,
or do we make the break?
What lies within the future,
if only we could tell,
then our choice would be easy,
we'd know the answer
could be heaven or hell.
But our fates are still a mystery,
and always will be so;
The question still remains,
do we stay or do we go?
So to the hills I would love to go,
to my cottage of dreams,
with its fires and oak beams,
to a new life of happiness
I'm sure we would know;
A more carefree life,
peace and content.
To the hills I must go,
I'm sure it is meant.

One journey north Brian wasn't feeling too good, so I took
over towing the car and caravan. This was my first attempt

at towing. All went well... when suddenly the whole caravan went into a snake... This felt like a giant shaking it! There was nothing I could do as the car veered up the embankment and we ended up facing the traffic coming towards us. The caravan had turned completely upside down on the ball joint and was a total wreck. The miracle was, there wasn't a scratch on the car. I jumped out of the car, crying my heart out... Police sirens sounded as the police arrived. They were so kind to me, making sure that we were both okay... saying that the caravan was replaceable, but people were not. Apparently, they had seen what happened: they were on the opposite side of the motorway when the accident happened, but couldn't do anything. They said the tyre had punctured... I had been blaming myself, but they assured me it wasn't my fault, just a punctured tyre that had written off Brian's caravan.

We were taken to the other side of the service area while they sorted out our wrecked caravan. The stress caused me to have a migraine. Eventually they towed our wrecked caravan on a trailer and it was locked in a compound with other wrecked vehicles. The next day we returned to salvage anything we could. The strangest thing was this: our small portable TV was dangling in mid-air and survived the crash! We loaded whatever was usable into our car and set off home from Toddington service area. Brian plugged the TV into a socket at home and miraculously it worked! Luckily we were well insured and the claim was promptly settled.

Maybe we should have called it a day, but Brian wanted another caravan, so off we went and bought another caravan. My parents thought we were mad at the time - maybe we were!

With Brian being a bad traveller, especially on coaches, caravanning was a good way for us to have holiday breaks with Shirley and Pickles. I was so soft with Pickles: I hadn't the heart to put him into kennels. (Being on a coach with Brian about to throw up at any moment wasn't my idea of fun either.)

We'd found out about Brian's travel sickness on a coach trip to Brighton for the day when we were courting. For a treat, I'd bought tickets for a couple of days at the sea; the first trip was to Brighton... and we ended up in the A&E at Brighton and Hove hospital and nearly missed the coach back home that night. The second trip to Eastbourne wasn't any better.

Although this happened years ago, it remained in my mind and I didn't want to chance going with him again on any coach trip! We did try a trip on the Green Line coach just from Old Windsor to Kingston one Saturday, and Brian was green by the time we got to Kingston. And that was just a one-hour journey. After that, any coach journey with Brian was out as far as I was concerned.

*   *   *

Just like our Queen, Brian and I had a *horribilis* year. My beloved father died in January, my best friend died in March, our daughter left home in September and my much loved dog, Pickles... left us for a higher place in the garden of the skies. (Pickle's demise left me broken hearted.) For anyone who's ever lost a dog, it's one of the worst bereavements to suffer. When you think about it, a dog is part of the family. Brian and I were on our own again... back to the two of us. In other words, 'The Empty Nest Syndrome!' I suppose it was another chapter in our lives. Parents have to face this at some time... not easy, but if you can let go of your children, just like a boomerang... they will come back. (Even if only for short visits.)

Our Queen had spoken of her *annus horribilis* - this was the year of the fire at Windsor Castle. We could see the Castle from our back bedroom window. We could see the sky lit up at night, flames climbing through the dense smoke... and this went on for days. We could not only see this, but smell it too although we were a few miles away as the crow flies.

Back to our situation: for holidays Brian and I tried hiring chalets, log cabins, etc., then he persuaded me to go down to the New Forest and have a look at the possibility of owning a mobile static caravan on a very nice site at Milford-on-Sea. In the end, after much persuasion, we bought a 26ft, two-bedroom static caravan and set it up as our holiday home. For anyone who's never been to The New Forest, it's delightful....

plenty of wild life and the ponies just wander freely wherever they choose. They have the right of way! After all, this is their home... we, the visitors, are the intruders!

I remember, for some reason we went down to the caravan very early one morning. We'd left home and were travelling through the village of Burley, and three young deer came from nowhere and disappeared into the woodland on a bend. It was such a privilege to see these animals, for they are very timid... We were so near to them as they pranced across the road within a few feet of the bonnet of our car. This is a rare sight, not seen very often. We were very lucky.

The site our caravan was situated on was very quiet... Woodpeckers were heard high in the trees. You could hear them pecking away at the tress, even if you couldn't actually see them. Jays flew around and are such beautiful colours. We often sat, just watching squirrels munching nuts that we put out for them. We got to know a few of the owners, but there wasn't any club site and the other owners weren't very friendly. We shopped in New Milton at the supermarkets, where again... the assistants weren't friendly.

We spent time walking down to the sea in Christchurch. We often drove through Boscombe town - approx. four miles of shops - and would sit near the cliff tops at Bournemouth, gazing out to sea. There were so many places to visit in the area, but we didn't really find the people friendly.

The journey from Windsor to the New Forest was approx. 80 miles, mostly motorway. We would get away on a Friday night. Sometimes the traffic was horrendous... especially around Winchester, where we often got held up. We returned home, often on a Sunday afternoon, because if we left later in the evening the traffic would be really bad. This all came to an end quite abruptly and unexpectedly. Brian was made redundant from his firm after 28 years of loyal service, and we had to sell the caravan. The money we got for it was a pittance, far less than what we'd paid for it.

*   *   *

Brian was just 52 years old, far too early to retire and get the state pension. Luckily, Brian was the FIRST man in the south of England to get a small pension from his firm. However this wasn't enough for us to live on, so something had to be done. We tried to sell our house in Windsor and buy a house in Ambergate, Derbyshire, which was suitable to run as a B&B. However, we couldn't sell our house... the market at the time was very bad for selling houses. That idea wasn't meant to be! Maybe it was a good thing we weren't able to sell our house, for it would have been very hard work running a B&B. I had no illusions on that score.

I remember lying awake at night, worrying what on earth we would do... How would we pay the bills, etc.? Things were so bad that we cashed in Insurance Policies. We couldn't afford to pay them and the money we got from surrendering them wasn't great... but every penny counted. Brian wanted to start up on his own in his capacity as electrician; however, I wasn't in favour of this... because with me being a secretary I knew I'd get landed with keeping the books! It was a bad time, with Brian applying for various jobs. During the next three years Brian filled in with different driving jobs. The third one ended up with him working twelve hours a day. We both hated this and he began applying for other jobs.

At long last he was offered a job as maintenance electrician with a shopping centre in nearby Slough. The salary was good and we thought he would be there until he was 65 and became eligible to draw the state pension. The irony of this was, after six years Brian was made redundant for the second time! They say 'lightening doesn't strike twice', but in our case it did!

Speaking of lightening, I think this happened the same year that Michael Fish, the weatherman, got it all wrong. We had gale force winds of around 90 miles per hour in Windsor! It was horrendous - terrifying, in fact. Brian was at work, so it was just myself and Pickles on our own. Outside we had some shutters either side of the windows. The wind blew one of ours down as well as one from our neighbour's house which flew across into our garden. Trees were being blown down in the gales, right across the country. The newspapers were full of horrendous photos, trees uprooted, severe damage to properties, power lines brought down, engineers working round the clock to restore power.

On another occasion, Brian was at work and we had a violent thunderstorm. I don't normally get upset by thunder and lightning, but this was different. Pickles was sprawled out in front of the electric fire when it happened. A bolt of lightning must have hit our chimney stack and a tongue of fire literally shot through the gap just underneath the fire, then retreated from whence it came. I'd never seen anything like it! Pickles shot up, his tail straight like a poker, his hackles raised in fear. If he could have spoken I'm sure he would have exclaimed, 'What the hell was that!' I was thinking the same thing.

Brian went down to the local job centre and was offered a job at a private school in Farnham Common. He accepted it just to get us through the winter... and he stayed for two years! Gradually, what began as a morning job had lengthened to full-time.

It was decision time again. Brian wasn't happy and we decided to put our house on the market and move. This was going to be tough: we'd lived in our house for 34 years and we now had a grandson. Hard as it was, though, we decided it had to be done. (For one thing our house needed a lot of money spending on it, money we just hadn't got.) But where would we move to... Devon or Derbyshire? Because I had relatives in Derbyshire, that's where we decided to go! Brian still had over two years before he was eligible to draw the old age pension.

This meant we had to allow a sum of money to live on for those two years... Brian was too old to look for work!

It's far from easy to find a property when it's as far away as Derbyshire, approx. 170 miles from Windsor. However, we began looking seriously for a bungalow around Easter time. We'd received details of a bungalow that looked just like the one we wanted. We booked a break in a static caravan near Buxton, Derbyshire, and made an appointment to view this bungalow. Although it was Easter, we had a snowfall, but this didn't deter us. The bungalow was the other side of Chesterfield, quite a distance from Buxton. Although it wasn't exactly what we wanted, we could both see the potential to make it into a lovely home, and we made an offer to the vendor.

On the way back to the site at Buxton, we ran into a white out. I thought it was fog, but Brian said 'It's snow.' I'd never seen anything like it before and felt scared. That night nine inches of snow fell! Even this didn't put us off the bungalow!

As soon as we got back to Windsor, we contacted our Estate Agent to place our house on the market. He did comment that our newly installed kitchen would sell our house, and he was correct. We were lucky in as much as two buyers wanted it badly, and one offered the asking price. We contacted our solicitor and put the wheels in motion. We had one or two blips before we finally exchanged, but exactly six months later we moved. During that long six months, I packed boxes, sorted out finances... Scraps of paper seemed endless as I made notes of everything involved in the move. Anyone who has ever moved house, which includes selling and buying a property, knows just how much stress this can be. Brian had given in his notice at the school and was home for the last month.

No wonder anyone will tell you that moving house and divorce are two of the most stressful events to go through! I did say to Brian, 'I only want to do this once!' I just hope we've got it right.

We'd said goodbye to everyone and it was the day of the move. Again, I had lists of paper, ticking away things to be done before we shut the door for the last time. It took four hours to pack our furniture onto the removal van. All we had to do now, was hoover through the house we were leaving, (this was on my list) and make sure everything looked clean and tidy before locking the door for the last time.

We got into our car, dropped the keys off with Robert, our Estate Agent and faced a long drive up the M1 to Derbyshire. Robert had become like a friend to us during the sale, and he hugged and kissed me goodbye.

Our furniture was by now on its way. We wouldn't be reunited with it until the next morning. Because of the long journey, the furniture went into a compound with the foreman for the night.

This was the beginning of our retirement - another chapter in our lives and another story!

*   *   *

I will write only a short synopsis, here, of the events that followed, since I've gone into great detail about 'Retirement' in a separate story!

Brian and I slept the first night in our new home, between two feather duvets breaking the hardness of the carpeted bedroom floor. It was rather like indoor camping, for we had no furniture, nothing to cook with and just enough food for breakfast... so long as it was just cereal. Anything else was off the menu, until we had the chance to go shopping.

Promptly at 9 a.m. our furniture arrived and the men began unloading. Two hours later, we had a double garage FULL of boxes, and a garden that resembled a garden centre... pots everywhere. Will we ever get straight, I began to wonder? Brian, the ever sensible Brian, merely said, 'We'll take one day at a time.'

This did work, (plus my never-ending pieces of paper, with lists of jobs to do). Will I ever discard my lists? I don't think so, it's just the way I am! At least I prioritise, and tick off as I go.

The first few weeks our phone constantly rang, old neighbours from Windsor wanting to know how we were getting on. The vendor we'd purchased our new home from called to collect his mail... remarking, 'You look as though you've been here for years - you should see the mess Joan and I are in!' We received many lovely cards wishing us well in our new home.

Brian had to quickly install a cooker circuit. We had an electric cooker and there was just a gas point in the kitchen. There were so many jobs to be done. (My lists were not only endless, they proved useful.)

We'd ordered a new fridge/freezer for the kitchen and this had to be filled. We'd brought a small freezer with us, which was out in the garage. This also, needed filling - so plenty of shopping to be done. The kitchen cupboards needed filling with food, too.

These first few weeks flew past. When we had time, I visited my relations who lived the other side of Derbyshire. We also trekked off down the M1 to see our daughter and grandson approx. every six weeks.

That old saying I'd heard so many times from different friends who'd retired - 'I don't know how I found time to go to work' - I could at last understand. We were now feeling exactly the same.

One or two friends came to stay and see our new home. (This was after we'd purchased a double divan bed for what we called 'our guest room'.)

My school friend and her partner came to stay with us a couple of times. I tapped on the bedroom door and discreetly asked if they'd like a cup of tea the first morning of their stay. They appeared from underneath the duvet like two naughty children, caught in the act! I hastily departed, closing the door quietly, whispering under my breath, 'Enjoy.'

I had offered to put the electric blanket on for them the night before... but was told by my friend's partner, 'I'll warm her up!' Seems like he was getting down to it! My mind went into overdrive imagining just how he was warming Joan up!

Visiting my relations in Derbyshire and trekking down the M1 to see our daughter and grandson, plus a lot of work in the garden and bungalow, all took a toll on Brian's health. He ended up in hospital for a few days. This was a warning, the doctors told us! Something had to be done... 'all work and no play,' etc.

Brian wasn't particularly energetic when it came to hobbies. He'd always enjoyed fishing, and snooker or billiards. We booked a couple of holidays in log cabins, situated around lakes so that Brian could fish. I was persuaded to try my hand at painting in oils. The two hobbies blended together quite well. I sketched and took photographs, then painted when we were back at home. Oils take a long time to dry, so are difficult to transport. I'd tried my hand with water colours, and didn't like the way they seemed to have a mind of their own. I wasn't in control and wasn't happy with that medium.

I'd begun to write poetry when I was in my thirties and found this relaxing... so much so, that I found my niche in writing poetry again. I found it flowed easily, almost like a telephone call into my brain.

Brian and I loved Scotland and booked a holiday in a log

cabin in Dumfries & Galloway. The peace and tranquillity of this remote site was a writer's haven. Even on a wet day, Brian drove round to the one and only shop for some newspapers and we settled down happily; elsewhere we'd both have been bored. We returned to Dumfries many times, always returning home relaxed. We visited Moffett and the Grey Mare's Tail, a real beauty spot. We both liked shopping in Castle Douglas. One real bonus in Scotland was the free parking, either in the car parks, or in the centre of the towns.

On our last trip to Moffett I had an accident, getting out of our car. I'd nearly done this so many times, but this particular day I managed to fall head first out of the car. I'd placed my handbag on the floor of our car in front of myself and caught my foot on the handle... and the next moment I was spread-eagled on the pavement with badly bruised and grazed knees Brian helped me up and we went back to our site. Even my trousers were torn and ruined... Silly me, but it did shake me up a bit.

These holidays had to be booked in advance, and because of health problems we had to cancel sometimes. What should we try next? Brian was a bad traveller on coaches, so that was not an alternative. I was okay, but it's no fun sitting with someone who's about to throw up at any minute. Should we try caravanning again? We'd spent many holidays in the past touring with a caravan. However, with age related aches and pains in various joints....maybe that wouldn't be a good idea. We then began to think of a campervan! Just climb aboard and drive. We found what we thought was the ideal camper for us and took the plunge and purchased it.

Our first trip out was horrendous! Clearly we hadn't thought it through enough. We really should have known better than to try and reach the south coast, approx. 250 miles from Derbyshire, for our first trip. Brian went along with my wish to see my old school friend who lived in Bognor Regis. (The friend who's partner warmed her up when they stayed with us!) We backed cautiously out of our driveway and off we went, planning to stop overnight at a caravan site near Henley... approx. halfway to Bognor. We didn't book in advance, (that was poor organization on our part). When we got to Henley, there was a festival on and the site was full! Oh dear, now what?

Brian merely said, 'We'll just carry straight on down to Bognor, but we'll stop for a bite to eat in Windsor Great Park!' My mind went blank. I thought, 'How the hell do we get to Windsor Great Park?' How ridiculous was that! I'd lived in Windsor for most of my life! Luckily Brian's sense of direction didn't falter. Although it was a Monday night and Windsor races were streaming out, we arrived in the park. I was worried about Brian driving 250 miles in one stretch at his age.

When we eventually arrived in Bognor it was dark and raining. We'd been on this site many times before with a touring caravan, so thought it would be easy to find. I was wrong! There were so many roundabouts - we literally went round in circles with Brian losing his temper! That didn't help... but at last we found the site and booked in. (Both of us were shattered by now.)

My friend Joan had said that they knew where the site was, and would come and see us when we'd arrived. I phoned her on my mobile, but she changed her tune and wanted us to go and visit them in the morning.

We sorted out the bedding for the night, but with rain pouring down ALL night we had very little sleep. The pitch wasn't level and by the next morning I wasn't feeling too good; in fact, I felt unsteady and nauseous. So, Brian was worried about me, and I was worried about him driving back to Derbyshire.

It was still pouring with rain and we still had to find Joan and Chris before we started back to Derbyshire. Joan had said the site was only a couple of minutes from their house - 'no problem then,' I thought. We packed things away and set off! Those roundabouts were everywhere! They appeared like mushrooms popping up. Oh dear... finally, with our nerves fraying I flagged a pedestrian down to ask the way. Luckily he knew the Avenue we were trying to find. If only Joan had kept her word it would have been so much easier for them to come to us. She was quite right when she'd said 'it's only a couple of minutes from here'! It was unbelievable just how near the site was. But then, Joan and Chris lived in Bognor and we didn't know the area.

At last we were in sight of their house. Brian turned the

camper round and we pulled up outside number 17! I was still feeling queasy, so Brian knocked on the door... explaining that I was unsteady and persuaded Joan to come and talk to me in the camper.

We hadn't seen each other for years and had a hug. Brian and Chris sheltered from the rain under their carport. I'd brought Joan's birthday gift, an oil painting I'd worked on for hours especially for her... It was of Burgh Island in South Devon. (It wasn't Joan's birthday for a couple of months, but I wanted her to have it and her birthday card.)

I never knew what happened between Brian and Chris; whatever it was caused the break-up of a 60-year friendship between Joan and me. I promised Joan I would phone her when we got back to Derbyshire, 250 miles away, which I did!

Brian and I decided to stop at a site in Oxford en-route and stayed for one night. Next morning we filled up this thirsty camper with petrol and headed for the M1 Motorway. A very quiet journey followed, the Motorway was busy and Brian needed to concentrate. Finally we arrived home, tired and shattered.

*   *   *

As promised a couple of days later I phoned Joan, who appeared to be a little frosty in her tone to me. To my utter surprise she accused Brian of being rude to Chris. As neither of us was present to hear exactly what was said, I decided to sit down and write to her in Brian's defence. I also sent her a postcard while we were away for a few days. She ignored my attempts at reconciliation. My own birthday passed a month before Joan's, and she didn't send me a birthday card. A month later on the day of Joan's birthday I plucked up courage and phoned her... this really did take some doing! I was utterly gobsmacked at her rudeness when she answered me. I said, 'Can't we draw a line under the whole business?' She merely said in a very stony voice, 'I think you've said it all.' She certainly wasn't going to let bygones be bygones. Over two years have now passed and I've sent them Christmas cards... all to no avail.

By the time two years had passed by, with no contact whatsoever between us. I'd got it all out of my system... WHEN the house opposite to our bungalow went up for sale. I didn't think much about it, until one afternoon I couldn't believe who I saw viewing it alongside the Estate Agent. YES, it was - Joan and Chris!

Time moved on and one day a Pantechnicon pulled up outside number 80 Gray Street, with me watching and waiting to see what our new neighbours looked like! Shock horror! Joan and Chris pulled up a little later in their car! I couldn't believe it! Joan and Chris living opposite....this would be awkward to say the least, after all my efforts at reconciliation!

Just then, I woke up... Thank God it was all a dream! (A nightmare!) I breathed a sigh of relief and went back to sleep.

*　　*　　*

Certainly, both Brian and I agreed the whole experience with the campervan hadn't been successful. Especially as my 60-year friendship with Joan had ended... not by us quarrelling, but by Brian and Chris having some disagreement!

Maybe we'd got it all wrong in attempting such a long maiden journey. Once we'd sorted ourselves out from that trip, I suggested to Brian that we try a local site for one night... Clumber Park in Nottinghamshire. Even this wasn't very successful. We had to agree that we'd bought the wrong camper and so - it had to go! We made a loss financially, but it was no use crying over spilt milk. Brian was like a dog with a bone and wouldn't give up on the idea of searching for the right model next time. The whole issue, (to me), was like stabbing my thumb with a very sharp knife... it hurt! The layout of that camper had been totally wrong; also, it was a petrol engine, which was very thirsty and expensive. However, I suppose we'd learned what to look for next time! I hoped so, anyway.

Sometimes you're in the right place at the right time... This is exactly what happened to us! Brian and I went to look at a camper which, when we viewed it, was much too large and unsuitable. Brian left me sitting in our car while he walked round the compound. He came back quite excited.... I thought to myself, 'Here we go again, I expect this is another waste of time!' However, I was wrong! The only thing I could find wrong with this camper was the price. Brian spoke to the Manager and between us we agreed a price suitable to our budget. Hurrah, mission accomplished!

This happened in December, but we both realised that if we didn't buy it, it was unlikely to still be there in the spring. So we decided to bite the bullet and go for it, although it wasn't the time of year to go camping. Roll on the spring, we thought!

During the long winter months we took the camper shopping sometimes... to give it a run. We didn't make the same mistake again and do a long run.

I suppose old memories die hard. It didn't seem to matter how many short runs we made, every time Brian suggested a NIGHT away in the camper, fear gripped my heart and my stomach lurched. In other words I felt physically sick! Oh dear, why had I started agreeing to buying another camper? Could I overcome my fears?

Dealers in the past had remarked that these types of campervans were what they called 'day vans'. To me, this was beginning to make sense now. Pity Brian wasn't convinced!

Some months later and still we hadn't slept overnight in the camper. Would we dare do it one day?

I'd persuaded Brian to 'take one step at a time' with short distances. Even the weather had warmed up and we could venture further afield. England, Scotland, Wales etc., these distant places could be our oyster now and we'd begun thinking, 'Maybe retirement isn't so bad after all.' But how long will it last? That's in the lap of the Gods.

PART THREE: SHIRLEY

My name is Shirley. I came into the world dramatically on March 26th, 1963. Georgie, my mother had wanted a baby so much, but for some unknown reason she and my father had been trying for four years before she finally became pregnant. (One neighbour joked about it, saying, 'Well, look at the fun you've had practising!'

I'm told that I was a wilful child, rather accident prone. Like the Saturday afternoon I fell in the garden... near where dad had fenced off a piece of garden with some wood stakes (to keep me off I suppose), but it was on the stakes I cut my head open! They didn't have a car at the time and phoned my grandfather, who raced up and carted me off to the nearest A&E. Apparently, I sat there laughing and chatting to the doctor while he stitched me up. I was three years old at the time.

Something else I couldn't get the hang of... getting food into my mouth! Luckily for me, Mother noticed my predicament and came to my rescue and she spoon-fed me. I liked my food, especially when I didn't have to try feeding myself. I really think I was a lazy child as well as a wilful one.

I always had grazed knees and bits of sticking plaster

somewhere. I think I should have been a boy, especially as I loved climbing trees. I loved having fun, and was always laughing. Maybe I was lazy too! I couldn't be bothered with all that learning to talk (like grown-ups). I found that I got what I wanted easily enough by pointing. Because of this I was carted off to hospital for a hearing test! The doctor thought I might be deaf, this being the reason for not talking. However the test proved that I wasn't deaf. Mother always seemed to understand what I wanted, so why couldn't others do the same? It proved a bit more difficult when I went to school though; they couldn't be bothered trying to understand me and suggested I went for speech therapy.

Mother would collect me from school and take me to the therapist. Some of the words he wanted me to practice were boring! 'Could I say 'sausages'?... of course I could say 'thausages' - nothing to it, but that was wrong of course. It took a while to get the hang of saying it correctly 'sausages'! Oh well, 'if you can't beat-'em, join-'em,' I laughingly thought to myself!

Although I was an only child, I wasn't a lonely child! I had friends before I went to school. They would come and play on my garden swing; also, Mother and I would go to their houses in the afternoons and while we played, our mothers would have a cup of tea and a chat.

I seem to remember I caught most of the children's ailments, even MUMPS! Now, my parents had never had mumps... I soon remedied that! I was generous and gave it to both of them the same weekend. They were well into their thirties, and I got sent off to Granddads'. I didn't mind, I had a fun time and enjoyed myself. (Even though I didn't feel too well.) I had plenty of lovely jelly and ice cream. It was almost worth having mumps. There's always a silver lining to everything!

I suppose I caught most ailments because my tonsils were really bad. I had tonsillitis so many times and drank so much pink antibiotics that I and my tonsils parted company in the end. I went into a place called 'hospital' to have them removed. A horrid woman called Matron, I believe, asked my mother, 'Is there anything Shirley doesn't like to eat?' To that my mother replied, 'Oh no, Shirley eats anything!' What she hadn't bargained for was MARMALADE on toast for breakfast. Now, I'd never tasted MARMALADE and spat it out! Oh dear... that didn't go down well with Matron. I didn't like her anyway. I think they were pleased to get rid of me and the next day I was sent home.

The hospital gave my mother a list of do's and don'ts and what to watch for. (Bright red bleeding, etc.) I could have fish-'n-chips to eat, that was good. All went well until the Sunday morning, when I woke up and my throat was bleeding... you got it, bright red blood! Mother phoned the doctor and I lay in bed waiting for him to come. It seemed such a long time before he turned up, so much so that when he did arrive I said to him, 'I could die waiting for you!' Well, he replied, 'You didn't, did you?' Oh dear, Mother wasn't pleased with me for saying that!

As I grew older I embarrassed Mother on many occasions by saying what I thought! Too bad, I thought, you get what you see with me! I certainly didn't want to grow into someone just like my mother, although everyone says that you do get like your parents as you grow older.

Although I was sent to a good school in Ascot, I can't say I enjoyed school very much. When I left, I had no 'O' or 'A' levels. I made some nice friends at school, but found schoolwork, homework especially, boring.

I was good at technical drawing and soon found a job in a builder's office. Three months later I left... It wasn't for me!

Mother passed on some advice given to her by her father: 'Get another job lined up before leaving the one you're in' - and I did just that.

I went for an interview in an office, nearby. I met a bloke there and we became quite friendly during lunch times - friendly enough for me to have morning sickness! Mother carted me off to see my doctor who, of course, asked the inevitable question: 'Are you pregnant?' I said, 'NO!' After three months of this sickness my periods resumed... Had I been lucky? That's for me to know and everyone else to guess! He was married - they always are if you like them! I didn't stay there for long before moving on again.

I was sixteen and going on holiday with my parents began to bore me. They were into caravanning, camping, etc., and I refused to go. They weren't very pleased with the thought of leaving me at home on my own, so the neighbours were all asked to keep an eye on me... I was threatened with the warning 'not to have any parties' - as if I would! Anyway, I decided to heed the warning for the sake of peace.

I began temping work and was never out of a job. It suited me; it wasn't boring because I was always somewhere different, working with different people. This went on for the next few years, until I was twenty-one... when I decided to leave home and branch out on my own. Again, this didn't go down well with my parents, who just couldn't understand that I wanted my independence. Oh well, as someone once said, 'You can't please all of the people all of the time... but only some of the people, some of the time!' Being me, I was only interested in pleasing *me*. I think that went down as me being selfish. (Very well, I *am* selfish - do you have a problem with that?)

I was going to live my life as *I* wanted, not as others wanted me to. I'd rented a room in a large old house just outside Windsor. The room had a very high ceiling and just an electric fire to keep warm (coin in the slot meter). At the end of each month money got tight, so it was early to bed to keep warm. My parents probably still couldn't understand me, BUT, I wanted my independence and I was determined to keep it now I'd got this far! I put my name down with a co-operative kind of place in Slough and very soon that's where I moved to. Privacy wasn't good there as it was communal living, so I put my name down on the

Council list for a flat. One became vacant in Maidenhead and, AGAIN, I moved on!

During these moves my parents were there for me, although they most probably didn't agree with what I was doing and how I was living.

The flat in Maidenhead was right at the top of the building - luckily there was a lift. (*When* it was working!) Mother and Father were very good and Father borrowed a white van to move my stuff one weekend. They managed to buy a second-hand baby belling cooker for me as a present. People were very kind and gave me pieces of furniture. I also asked Mother if I could have my old bed, to which they said 'yes'. This was good; it made me feel happy sleeping in the bed I'd slept in before I left home.

My parents helped me set up my new home. At least they didn't bear me any grudges! I even had proper heating here... no more going to bed to keep warm, BUT it was expensive! Before I realised it I was in money trouble with my bank! Stupidly, I kept this to myself and said nothing.

Sometimes it was lonely being on my own, so I decided to join the 18-30's club. It was here that I met Richard and Dave, amongst many others. It seemed that Dave fancied me, whilst I fancied Richard. There was a bank holiday coming up and it seemed the 18-30's club were going to a coastal site for the few days. This was my chance: I quickly booked my place with the others... It was in two months' time to be exact. During those two months Richard and I became an item... We bonded together, so well, that we slept together during the bank holiday.

Shortly afterwards I'd been advised by my dentist to have my four wisdom teeth extracted because they were impacted. Trust me to have difficult teeth, which had to be extracted in hospital. It was while I was in hospital that Richard met my parents for the first time. (Until then they didn't know he existed.) Oh well, there I was looking like a hamster, face all swollen and parents shaking hands across the bed with Richard.

It was with Richard I shared my debt problem with the bank, and not my parents. I got myself out of trouble by leaving the flat and going into a rented room in another part of Maidenhead. To cut a long story short, it didn't work! My parents came to visit me and even invited me to go back home until I sorted myself out. My stubborn streak and pride prevented me from accepting that offer and instead I went to live with Richard in his basement flat in Reading. This was a typical bachelor pad, but I loved him, so it didn't matter much that it was a damp, dingy place. I'd got what I wanted.

One day Richard said to me, 'If we're still together in five years' time, I'll marry you.'

'Is that a proposal?' I asked, thinking to myself, 'I'm not waiting five years - you'll have to speed things up a bit!'... but I said nothing.

Right from the start, Richard had made it clear that he didn't want children. I changed his mind on that score,

BUT we didn't want children out of wedlock and so we got married. (Long before the five years was up!)

Because neither of us was religious, we got married in Reading Registry Office. My best friend was my Matron of Honour, and Richard's best friend was his Best Man. We had a reception at a country PH near Marlow, Bucks. Luckily for me my parents paid for this. (After all, by now it was ten years since I left home.) They did stipulate, however, that if I wanted a disco, it would be at our expense... which it was. However, everyone went back to my parents for toasts of wine, and we cut a beautiful wedding cake which they'd had made for the occasion. We had the speeches from Richard and his Best Man... and everything went swimmingly.

All this had taken time to arrange, with a few disagreements between Mother and myself on the phone. I remember one night shouting at her on the phone: 'Whose wedding is it?!' This is one of my faults, you see - I say what I think and hang the consequences, something that doesn't always go down well! I know that I should think before I speak, but I tend to open my mouth and out it comes... no matter who I upset.

Richard and I went to Cyprus for our honeymoon. After we returned, we talked things over and decided to move nearer to our places of work... Maidenhead. The flat in Reading was put on the market, but this was now in negative equity and it cost us a lot to move. We bought a four bedroom mid-terraced house near to Maidenhead town centre. It had an extension added in the loft space with an en-suite bathroom. We thought we were very lucky to get it at a price within our budget. To help with the mortgage payments, I heard of someone where I worked who was looking for a bedsit... She was single, and went home at weekends. It all worked out quite well.

Once settled, we began trying for a baby, and very soon I became pregnant. We had it all worked out. I would have the baby, take maternity leave and place him/her in a nursery. When we told my parents our plan, Mother said, 'If that's what you plan to do, why have a baby? You'll miss out on so much.' She really couldn't understand us at all! It was a different way of life in their day... When a baby came along, the mother stayed at home to look after it. Anyhow, this is what we planned to do regardless of what anyone else said. All our friends were doing the same thing - it was the modern way of life.

My parents had a mobile static caravan on a site in the New Forest, and we persuaded them to let us have a weekend down there. It was there that I conceived! Much later I told Mother that I'd conceived that weekend, and she said, in a shocked tone, 'You did *that* in *our* caravan?!'

They didn't let us borrow it again because I teased them, saying, 'I think we'll keep the keys for another time!' That didn't go down well. (I really should learn when to keep it zipped!)

Robert, our baby boy, was born on the 27th January by

caesarean section. He was a bouncing 10lb bundle of joy. Richard was at the birth and even took photographs in the delivery room. Mother and Father came to see Robert the next day. I was in hospital for some days afterwards. There was snow on the ground when we took him home.

Robert was a hungry baby - I always seemed to be feeding him. Mother advised me to top up his bottle... but I'd been told a baby mustn't have anything but milk for the first three months. As usual, Mother disagreed, saying that he needed something more solid, a little egg yolk, etc., for starters. 'It didn't do you any harm,' she added, 'and you were a big baby.' I kept my thoughts to myself for once and said nothing.

Richard and I wanted to go to the Theatre Royal when Robert was three weeks old, and I asked my parents if we could drop him off at their house and go? They agreed to have him. After all, he was bottle fed, so he shouldn't be any trouble. I think Mother had been walking Robert up and down with him over her shoulder and was pleased when we arrived back. She'd fed him, burped him, changed him... all to no avail! Robert just wanted his mum, and where was she? Gone to the Theatre! Oh well, it was not going to stop us going out together, so they might just as well get used to it. 'After all, that's what grandparents are for, isn't it?' That was my opinion anyway!

I was keen to get back to work, and placed Robert in a local nursery. It had always been my intention anyway, and I wasn't going to put my life on hold. Life, after all, is for living. My parents didn't agree with this I knew... Just too bad I thought, it's my life!

For the first three years of Robert's life, Mother and Father babysat for us regularly... and we were grateful. The strange thing was, whenever they babysat for us... Robert slept well. We joked about it. Father said he'd got a rubber hammer... I asked to borrow it! They slept the night at our house sometimes if we were going to be really late home. He was no trouble to them, whereas with us he'd wake several times in the night crying normally. I noticed that when Mother changed Robert's nappy and got him ready for bed, he didn't struggle for her. He seemed to be a different child when they were in charge. We were getting ready to go out one night, and while Father was drying Robert on the bathroom floor, he lay there as good as gold. I said to him, 'You don't lie there for me like that!' Father replied, 'You don't know how to handle him!'

Father had been made redundant after working 28 years for his company. It was a shock to them for until recently a man worked for a firm until he retired. He'd taken other jobs after this, but stayed for about two years in each one.

Then, they dropped the bombshell... They put their house on the market and prepared to move 170 miles north to Derbyshire! Richard said, 'Don't worry, they won't go... they've been on about moving for years.' BUT what we didn't know was that their house needed work doing on it and they simply hadn't got the money for the repairs.

They did move, and I really thought they'd done it to spite us and I was angry! How could they move so far away from me, and Robert, their only grandson? One day we were speaking on the phone and I overheard Mother shout at Father: 'She hates us for what we've done... moving up here!' What they didn't know was... Richard and I were planning on having another baby. They moved to Derbyshire in the September, and by November I was pregnant. Although they visited us at six-week intervals, I said nothing until the Christmas. When I did tell Mother I was pregnant, she said over the phone, 'Well, you're either very brave or mad, after the time you had giving birth to Robert!' And she added: 'And we won't be around to babysit so easily.' I said, 'That's okay, we'll muddle through' - and we had to, somehow.

We didn't see my parents' bungalow until the March... they'd been moved in for six months by then. I said to them, 'I love the bungalow, but I would have preferred it if it had been in Alstonefield.' Mother replied, 'So would I, but we couldn't afford it had it been in Alstonefield!' and she added, 'There's always a compromise Shirley, and this is the only compromise.'

Richard was, and always had been, a naturist. I don't think my parents realised this for a long time... This made things awkward, and we didn't often stay with them. They still came down regularly to see us and Robert.

In the August of that year I gave birth to Louise. I

discharged myself from hospital since I wasn't going to stay in there, being told what to do and what not to do. Mother and Father came down to see Louise. Things were a bit chaotic: I'd had another rough birth and the nurse came in to see me daily. I got an infection where I was stitched; maybe it was my own fault for not bathing as much as I should have done. Ah well, I'll live. No sympathy from Richard. 'One has to die to get any sympathy from him,' I told Mother.

Gradually the visits became less frequent. I went back to work and Louise went into nursery, just the same as Robert had done. Whenever they did visit, we made the most of it and went off out somewhere. One night, just before we went out, Richard was talking about where we'd go the next evening. I knew by Mother's face that he'd said the wrong thing... and the next morning they went back to Derbyshire! Oh well, it was nice while it lasted! One day Richard might learn to keep it zipped!

Whenever we could, we'd take off down to Studland Bay in Dorset. Father twigged on quickly that it was a naturist site. Mother kept on asking what the attraction to Studland Bay was. I kept fobbing her off, until a programme came up on TV about it... then I had to admit they'd been correct all along: YES, it was a naturist site. I said to Mother, 'What's wrong with taking your clothes off?' She merely replied, 'Each to his own!' But I could tell she wasn't thrilled about it. Oh well, it's our life and we'll live it the way we want to. I'm not a child any more.

The years went by and Richard's department where he worked closed down, and he was made redundant. His firm offered him a job at their other depot in Stowmarket, Suffolk. We put our house on the market and it took over a year to sell. It was a nice house, but we hadn't done much to it and Richard wanted top dollar for it. We were so desperate to sell it, though, that we had it listed with four estate agents at one time. Mother suggested to Richard that the problem was the entrance; she advised him what would make it more attractive... A few coloured slabs laid down and some pots of flowers or small conifer trees. (Which we could take with us.) But he wouldn't listen to advice from anyone. She bluntly told him that if she was looking to buy any house and the front looked like ours, she'd tell Father to drive straight on. She said, 'I wouldn't even get out of the car and look inside!' He merely grinned, thinking she was talking rubbish. But, she was correct... presentation was the all-important factor in selling a property. (They didn't have a problem selling their house, so she did know what she was talking about.) Richard may have a PhD, but when it came down to common sense, he was blinkered. After all, Mother was correct... You have to get a buyer through the front door if you ever want to sell a house!

Eventually we did sell our house, and moved to Suffolk. The dormer bungalow was one of nine different properties we viewed one Sunday. By the end of the day, I really didn't know which one we'd bought. This proved obvious, for when

I went back to finalise details... I'd thought the bathroom was blue. It was pink! The kitchen was green, and not at all as I remembered it. Oh well, hopefully this will be our home for a long time to come. It was very quiet in comparison to our house in Maidenhead... and we had to find our way round the country lanes which all looked the same!

Suffolk seems to be a very affluent county, expensive housing, food, etc. I persuaded my parents to come down and see our house before I found a job. They did a quick visit during the first fortnight after we moved. Oh dear... Mother told someone when they returned home to Derbyshire that there's more life in a graveyard! The only bit of excitement she said 'was if a horse passed by'!

Finding a place of work wasn't easy either. Richard had his job, but vacancies for clerical work were like searching for gold. I tried signing on with agencies; they found me a couple of jobs which were unsuitable and I quickly left. It took a few months before I found something really suitable.

Life was now getting back to normal for us all. The kids were settling down at their schools and I was settling down nicely in my new job and found some new friends. They were a nice bunch of girls. Richard seemed to like his job and cycled to work each day in all weathers. He, too, had found friends, and they met sometimes at night for a game of badminton. He's the energetic type.

We soon found a nice naturist beach, which we visited whenever we could. My parents came to visit when they found time. Although they were retired in Derbyshire, both had hobbies. Father liked fishing, Mother took up writing seriously now she had more 'me time' to do it. She also began painting in oils.

They booked log cabins for short breaks about an hour's drive from where we lived. They visited us in the evening time. All was going well when a disaster came which neither Richard nor I had foreseen. The department where Richard was working closed down and once again Richard was made redundant! Luckily for us, he was given a good redundancy deal which enabled us to pay off our mortgage... but he still had to find another job.

Richard was offered a good job, BUT it was in Letchworth... 55miles away from where we lived. We didn't want to move again, so he decided it would be better for him to commute. More expense since he needed a car for this journey.

Richard was now away from home 12 hours a day, and driving 110 miles daily back and forth. At least we both had jobs again, but again I was to learn the truth of the dictum, 'Never count your chickens before they've hatched!'

I went into work one day to be told to get my things together and in just a short matter of time... I was AGAIN made redundant! That day, when I got home, I was in shock! So it was back to applying for work for me. I knew this wouldn't be easy!

(During this time, and much to my surprise, Mother told

me, 'I know you thought I was hard on you as a child, but I'm proud of the way you've handled being made redundant.')

Once again I joined a temping agency. All I could find to suit my CV was an evening job. Beggars can't be choosers, so I took it. The next crunch came at Christmas... Richard's company had lost contracts and there were more redundancies, including him! He was offered another job, different to what he'd been doing... so another skill for him to learn. The distance for him to travel was the same as before.

A few months later I applied for a morning vacancy for an audio typist - something I'd never done before. However, I got the job! This was a good move for me: it was nearer to home... plus, I had more money coming in. It was hard going, but I soon got the hang of it and balanced the two jobs well.

There is nothing certain in today's job world as I soon found out once again. I went into work on the Monday evening... to be told that they'd lost two contracts and my services would no longer be required by the end of the week! Oh well, I thought, it's a good thing I have my morning work! The very next morning, Tuesday... I was told I wasn't suitable. In just two days and I'd lost both jobs! So, back to square one, job hunting again.

To qualify for any benefits I have to sign on each week and also look for, and apply for, any jobs that I'm capable of doing. (That's the law.) We're off to France in a few weeks' time for our annual holiday. Because of this I can't see anyone wanting to employ me straight away, so for the time being I'm enjoying my home and reading in the garden, also camping at weekends. After all, I must get my priorities right: '...all work and no play etc.'

I had to attend three interviews before going to France. This was on the day before we went. To my surprise I was offered a temporary post until Christmas. They wanted me to start straightaway, BUT were willing to wait until I'd been to France. So when I return, I begin work the very next day. (That's unless they find someone else better qualified, who isn't going on holiday.) I'll have to wait and see what happens on that score.

For the time being, I'm off to France and will forget everything else and enjoy myself... After all, that's what life's about, having fun and enjoyment!

I always said I would never get like my mother! She's too fussy for my liking, things have to be in their place, she's orderly, very meticulous and has to do things a certain way. Not me... I get my priorities right, a good book to read, a bottle of wine, chocs and candles to relax with! Things like cleaning, housework, etc., get done when I feel like it. Life is about having a good time! Mother is far too serious... She's methodical, she writes poetry and stories. I read - she writes! How could I ever become like her? I broke with family tradition by giving birth to Robert and Louis. My mother was an only child... and I am an only child too! But, then again... Father told me I'm like *his* mother, my other grandmother. I'm not sure if that's a compliment or not!

I do know that next year I'll reach the big 50! WOW, what a celebration that will be! Get saving, Richard, you don't know what you're in for! My birthday bash is likely to go on for at least a week or two... maybe longer!

RETIREMENT

PREPARING FOR 24/7

Retirement… is similar to when the kids flee the nest; it's another stage in life. What will this final stage in life bring forth? (When you're past your sell by date, as it were?)

Happiness, heartache… whatever it may be, combine it with a little divine intervention, and: 'You'll cope!'

I did, and I'll tell you all about it, and I'm still coping… BUT, as with everything in life, 'The grass isn't always greener.'

I realise that getting old means one has more memories to recall than years to look forward to. However, it's not all downhill, it does have some advantages. A free bus pass at the age of 60. Super saver vouchers for visiting the cinema and, once over the age of 75, a FREE TV LICENCE for life!

*   *   *

How often have you heard someone say 'I don't know how I found time to go to work'? It's not until you, yourself, are retired, that you believe this statement!

Maybe, it's because as we get older… we slow down.

Simple tasks take us longer to perform. Old age stealthily creeps upon us, almost unnoticed. When you're in your thirties, mid-forties... you don't think you'll ever get old. In fact, you don't think about age much, you're too busy enjoying life. But if you're lucky, you will reach old age quicker than you realise.

Our retirement came a little earlier than we'd planned, forced upon us by redundancy. It was the second redundancy that was the final crunch. We dealt with the blow by moving away from the house we'd called our home for thirty-four years, moving 170 miles north.

This was a hard decision, for just three years earlier we'd been blessed with our first Grandchild.

We'd spent many holidays and short breaks in our caravan, touring the country... dreaming of retiring one day to our haven. (Dreams don't always materialise, but ours did.) We were divided between Devon and Derbyshire... both beautiful counties. We chose Derbyshire because of family ties.

Finally after months of packing and saying goodbye to our friends, we locked the doors for the last time and handed the keys to our Estate Agent. He hugged me and kissed me goodbye. He'd become like a friend to us.

Because of our familiarity with this beautiful County we took to it like 'ducks to water'.

The first night of our adventure began with us sleeping on the floor between two feather duvets. At least this softened the hardness of the carpeted floor. The journey North was long, and our furniture was safely locked in a compound overnight under the care of the Foreman of the removal team. This was due to arrive around 9 a.m. the next morning.

We were touched by what we thought was a lovely gesture. The Vendor left a card on the windowsill wishing us happiness in our new home. (This had been their home for the past 17 years.) Also, neighbours either side had left cards of welcome for us, their new neighbours. Our new adventure had now begun. From when we'd placed our house on the market, it had taken nine months to get to this stage. At long last, what had begun as a dream had materialized into reality. Let's hope we've done the right thing. Only time would provide the answer to this.

Tomorrow was time to make a start on transforming this property, a modern bungalow, into our HOME!

Before we settled down, though, we carried our Aquarium indoors... plus our aquatic fish. Removal men won't carry livestock and so we'd done the best we could to keep them warm while we journeyed the 170 miles north. We were lucky - we only lost just one fish. Remarkable really, as fish are known to die with noise and vibration, which they'd certainly endured on the journey. The next part of our new life began early the following morning.

*   *   *

We were up early the next morning and made a cup of tea on our camping stove, then ate our breakfast cereals. Thankfully the weather was fine at this stage. The removal men arrived promptly and began unloading our furniture.

The double garage was soon full of boxes. The garden took on the look of a garden centre. The furniture was very nearly unloaded when the heavens opened and torrential rain cascaded down, amid... thunder, lightning - what a welcome! The removal men just stood around for about half an hour. There was nothing else they could do but wait for the storm to subside.

Hours later, we were on our own... and I'm wondering, 'Will we ever get straight?' John, my ever sensible husband, merely made us another cup of tea and remarked, 'We'll take one day at a time now.' And I had to agree that was all we could do. After all, I thought, we've got all the time in the world now we're FINALLY retired!

Later on in the day our new fridge/freezer was delivered. All we had to do was let it stand for 24 hours, then find some shops and fill it up.

The first week in our new home just flew past. We busily unpacked all those boxes in the garage so that our car could be safely garaged.

My cooker was electric... no cooker circuit. (Good job John was an electrician!) We'd brought a new microwave with us and I managed to cook with that, plus just one ring of my cooker. If I'd used more than one ring, it would have blown the fuses. After all, there's more than one way of skinning the cat. (Another well-known proverb!) We managed. We filled the cupboards with food and John soon ran a cooker circuit.

Hallelujah! We're getting more organized daily.

Ray, the previous owner, called round to collect his mail. He sat down, looked around and remarked, 'You look as though you've been here for ages. You should see the mess Joan and I are in!'

Later that night John looked at me and said, 'I feel as though we've been here for years.' I thought to myself, 'It's going to be okay, we've done the right thing, no doubt about that!'

A neighbour called round to welcome us, the new arrivals, and brought us a small book containing the history of this small village. I found it so interesting. In the book were details stating that some of the original inhabitants were of the name Richardson! I was aghast when I read this. My maiden name is Richardson. Was this the reason I'd felt that I'd come home? Fate has a habit of strange coincidences and happenings throughout one's lifetime!

*   *   *

Phase two of our journey into Retirement.

All the months that we were in the process of moving, I wrote lists. Pieces of paper were strewn everywhere... and now, here I am ensconced in our new home and, YES, I'm still writing lists. This time for jobs to be done, prioritizing as I go. It's the only way I know. Organization is the way forward, it's my way!

For the first few months we gradually sorted out what had to be done, which kept us busy. We had brought many cans of paint and John gradually worked his way through them. Luckily for us, all our furniture fitted... even our curtains that I'd had professionally made before we moved north which fitted the windows with no alterations needed. This again, was proof that this bungalow was meant to be our new home. How often can anyone move home with furniture and curtains that fit perfectly?

Although our new home was perfect for us, everyone compromises in some way when they move, it's the only way. We could both see the potential in this bungalow and now we'd begun putting our ideas into practice it was getting better every week.

For instance, the kitchen had green cupboards. (We had left a beautiful kitchen in our house down south - I knew this was one compromise.) I thought I could live with these green cupboards, but three months later I had to admit... 'I was wrong.' Something had to be done. We needed a carpenter and asked neighbours for advice, preferring to go with recommendation rather than resort to the Yellow Pages.

We obtained a quote from a local tradesman, who ordered our chosen units. In just two days of work, Peter revamped the kitchen. What a difference! It was completely transformed... and without breaking the bank. For once I kept right out of the way (this was hard for me) instructing John to keep Peter happy with mugs of coffee.

We were making headway, creating a home again. Besides working hard on the interior alterations, we needed to give attention to the garden... which was a blank canvas. Now, luckily, I'm 'green fingered'. The garden certainly needed someone to love it, nurture it and tend it.

We tried to have one day out each week for relaxation. 'All work and no play make Jack a dull boy' (another proverb). We made regular visits to see my relations who lived the other side of Derbyshire. Our garden was shaping up well, but I wanted to build a rockery and my Aunt had plenty of wonderful rock stones which she gave us freedom to take, whatever we wanted. I bought plants, bulbs, shrubs, conifers and miniature fir trees. A few passers-by noticed my efforts and kindly dropped off small bags of plants which I gratefully accepted.

We really did take on a project when we bought our bungalow. It was a challenge... but we loved this challenge. This had been our dream all our married life, to own a bungalow, and at long last we'd achieved it.

Our daughter and grandson were still 170 miles away down south, so every six weeks we went trekking off down the M1 to visit them. I missed them of course... we'd only lived six miles apart before our move North. We were quite busy. Now I knew just how true it was when people had told me, 'I don't know how I found time to go to work' - I hadn't believed them at the time, but now we were retired ourselves, and, YES, it was true!

That Christmas, three months after we moved north, our daughter told us she was pregnant again… and the following August our granddaughter Emma was born. Now we had two grandchildren to visit down south. Because of her being pregnant, it was six months before our daughter came to visit and see our bungalow. (During this time John and I continued trekking off down the M1.)

All this took a toll on John's health and he ended up in hospital for a short spell. The neighbours were very kind to me, ferrying me back and forth to see John in hospital. I nursed him back to health gradually over the following months. This was a warning, the doctors told us!

This was one of the first lessons in coping with retirement. Things don't always run smoothly, but, remember to work together. After all, when you marry, you take each other 'for better, for worse, in sickness and in health'. These bad times test your strength to the limit. What doesn't kill you, makes you stronger! (Another well know proverb!)

With age comes wisdom. We had to slow down our pace somehow.

The next step was to take up some hobbies - another step in the right direction!

*   *   *

Phase three of our journey into retirement.

We both had time on our hands for the first time in years.

For myself, I'd always envied anyone who could paint. (I don't mean walls!). At last I now had an opportunity to have a go at artwork. John had always loved fishing and when we lived in the south, he would go off down to the river Thames on his day off work. Now we could combine both hobbies. John could fish and I could paint! To be honest, fishing bored me, so if I painted while John fished, this could be the perfect answer.

While John had fishing gear, (stored up in the loft since we moved) I had no artwork materials at all. My birthday was coming up and John suggested he buy me a basic kit to get me started.

Many people begin painting in watercolours. I tried this medium, but it wasn't for me. What I didn't like about this medium was that it appeared to have a mind of its own! I wasn't in control and didn't like this feeling. A neighbour suggested to me, 'Why don't you try painting in oils?' John then bought me a basic set of oil paints and set of brushes.

I soon found this was just what I wanted. If I made a mistake, or didn't like something... with oils it was easy to correct, I could paint over my mistake.

With our new found hobbies, we booked ourselves a holiday break in a log cabin beside a lake. John sat fishing while I sketched away, then eventually painted what I'd sketched and taken photographs of. Because oil paints take a while to dry and are not easy to transport, I painted at home. There's often a compromise to anything, and this was the case with painting in oils. One had to be patient… I'd now found my hobby taught me patience and was very relaxing. While I sat for many hours painting, everything else was driven from my mind.

For some reason, I began writing poetry and prose; this also rid me of unwanted worries and problems. I also found that if something or someone upset me in any way, writing a piece of poetry or a short story removed the anger from my system. In other words, this proved a way of relaxation for me. I only had an electric portable typewriter at this stage, which I'd bought from a friend. Even this was the very first electric typewriter I'd ever worked with… my experience with typewriters went back to when I was a secretary with an ancient Remington that rang a bell at the end of each line, a push handle to move to the next row… and of course the messy job of changing its ribbon. I was on the up, BUT nothing lasts for ever and after a couple of years my electric typewriter required some costly repairs. What could I do now?

In the meantime I'd joined a local Business Enterprise company and the Coach suggested I get a COMPUTER! As I knew nothing about computers, Jack was a great help to me - he knew what he was doing and ordered it for me online. He'd said, 'I taught my father, who's 70 to use one, so I can teach you'… so began another new venture for me. I didn't even know how to switch it on for starters, but Jack was a good teacher and taught me the basics. Gradually, over a period of time, I even began to like my computer. (Whereas for starters I was afraid of the beast!) So here I go again, at the age of approaching 70, I'm learning about computers! Even at such a late stage of life, I could still learn something new.

I still had to cook, shop, attend to my plants in our garden, do ironing and endless tasks; occasionally we would have a drive into the glorious Derbyshire countryside and fit in a break to see our daughter and grandson. Life was very busy... what I'd been told all those years ago, really sunk in now: 'I don't know how I found time to go to work!' And to think I didn't believe the people who'd told me this! Now I did! I'd not been so busy in years. What would the next stage bring forth?

*   *   *

Phase 4 of our journey into retirement.

John and I planned some holidays; we both liked Log Cabins on quiet sites. We'd found a lovely site in Dumfries & Galloway, Scotland. This turned out to be the perfect environment for writing... I penned five pieces of poetry there. The peace and tranquillity was awesome. At the end of our stay I'd not felt so relaxed in many years and said to John, 'We'll have to return here again, and not leave it too long.' Life has a way of being awkward sometimes. We did return a few years later; in the meantime we'd both endured health problems and had cancelled bookings because of this. Now we had to think of some other means of having holiday breaks.

In our younger years we'd spent many years touring the country with our touring caravan, and we wondered, should we get another caravan? That way we could come and go more easily. The snag to this idea was the fact that with ageing years, we both had joint pain... arthritis, etc., so pushing and shoving a caravan into place wasn't the answer. John wasn't too good at reversing either, if we happened to take a wrong turning... even with all the years we'd toured with a caravan on the back of our car, he hadn't improved this technique, so back to the drawing board!

John had always been a bad traveller on coaches, so going on a coach tour was out of the question. I was okay, but being with someone about to throw up at any moment was not my idea of fun!

The best idea seemed to be... a campervan! John had driven cooker wagons when he worked, so no problem with driving a large vehicle. The problem with this idea was space on our driveway. We started looking around compounds for a reasonable size campervan. Many didn't have a toilet compartment, which was a priority as far as I was concerned. With age comes visiting the loo in the night... and so I put my foot down if there was no toilet. The larger campervans were more luxurious and had the toilet compartment... BUT our driveway wasn't large enough to accommodate one of those. Oh dear... this was proving more difficult than either of us imagined it would.

After searching for around two seasons, we eventually found (what we thought) was the perfect little camper for us. One of the first trips out with it proved disastrous; I'll explain why, because that is another story!

*   *   *

We loaded up the camper with essentials, a few clothes, toiletries, some food etc., then backed off with caution from our driveway. We were heading for the south coast (approx. 250 miles in distance), to visit an old school friend. We'd planned to stop overnight on a caravan site near Henley on Thames. Alas, we hadn't booked in advance and didn't know there was a festival on that weekend... site full up! Oh dear, now what?

John said, 'We'll drive through Windsor, to Windsor Great Park, have a bite to eat... then continue our journey.' I was worried at this point that 250 miles at John's age would be too much strain on him as the only driver. Certainly I couldn't drive the camper.

Driving through Windsor proved a nightmare. It was some years since we'd been to Windsor and everything seemed to have changed. New blocks of flats had sprung up everywhere. Shock horror, today of all days and it was Windsor races, and they were streaming out. I was feeling terrified by now. So terrified, in fact, that my mind went blank as to how we could get to Windsor Great Park. Good job John seemed to get to grips - eventually we were in the Park.

We parked the camper off the road where it was quieter, then sorted out some food and a drink of tea before setting off again. By this time the roads were busier - we'd hit the time when the work force were on their way home. Eventually we got near to Guildford, slowly advancing towards open country. Many miles further on, through seemingly endless villages it was now getting dusk. We were making for a caravan site at Bognor Regis. We'd stopped there many years before when we had a touring caravan... no problem, we thought. However with the light fading, we just went round in circles with John and I getting more and more frustrated as time went by. At last we found it and paid our fee for the night. It was now beginning to rain.

All we had to do now was sort out the bed and get undressed. I phoned my friend on my mobile phone and asked if they would come round in the morning... (She'd already said they knew just where the site was and it wouldn't be a problem, just two minutes from their house). However, it was a different story now we'd arrived... she insisted we went to their house.

We then settled down for sleep... it poured with rain

incessantly ALL night. (Have you ever tried to sleep with rain pounding on a metal roof? It was nothing short of impossible!) The next morning, I wasn't feeling at all well. Not getting much sleep and the camper not being on level ground, I felt somewhat unsteady on my feet, a little nauseous. Not looking forward to the day ahead... it was still pouring with rain, and we'd still got 250 miles to get back to Derbyshire.

We washed, dressed and showered at the club site shower block, had some breakfast and set off to see my friend. John was worried about me and the fact that I was unsteady on my feet. Again we got lost in Bognor, it had so many roundabouts... we just went round in circles. Luckily I managed to flag down a pedestrian and ask the way... and at last we found my friend's house. If only she had kept her promise and come to us... because it was barely two minutes' drive for them, and they knew the way whereas we didn't.

With the rain still pouring down, John said, 'You stay in the camper, I'll get Joan to come out and you can talk together.' John rang the doorbell, and Joan and Chris came out. Joan climbed into the camper. I gave her a hug as well as her birthday present and card. We sat and talked while John and Chris took shelter from the rain.

Neither Joan nor I ever knew what happened between the men, but Joan was none too pleased that we didn't go inside. Chris, apparently, had tried to direct John along a different route back to our home, not the one we knew...

and John refused to try this because he wasn't familiar with Chris' directions. I told Joan that I would phone her when we got back home.

I kept my word and a few days after we got back home I rang Joan, but she didn't sound very friendly and accused John of being rude to Chris. This upset me and I tried to explain that John was merely worried about me... I was feeling unwell and he knew we had a long journey home. I wrote Joan a letter of explanation. I sent her a card the next time we had a short holiday... all to no avail. (Deafening silence from Joan.) All this upset me because Joan and I had been school friends nigh on 60 years, yet she ignored my attempts at reconciliation. It was Joan's birthday in September so I plucked up courage and phoned her. I was gobsmacked to say the least at her rudeness to me and the fact of her unwillingness to forgive and forget. (We'd always been like sisters, and her attitude hurt.) So, a 60-year friendship ended, not by us having a quarrel, but by the two men in our lives. (Anyway, now I'll go back to when we left Joan and Chris.)

After leaving Joan and Chris I said to John, 'I'm not wanting to do the whole journey in one go, so where can we pitch on the way home?' He said, 'We'll make for Oxford and stop the night at Woodstock.' This again was a site we'd often used with our caravan.

We pulled in, paid our site fee and drove round to the allocated pitch. It was such a different night, quite warm and pleasant. We wandered over to the toilet block, showered, etc., and much later we began the task of sorting out the bedding and settling down for sleep. Thankfully it wasn't raining.

This camper wasn't proving ideal for sleeping. It had a double bed, so we had to clamber over one another to reach the toilet in the night. The bed was made up from side to side... not ideal as one couldn't stretch out fully. This was one fault we hadn't spotted when we purchased it. It was also a 2.0 petrol engine... which proved expensive. We seemed to be forever filling up en-route. I was beginning to have doubts as to whether this was the right camper for us after all.

Next morning we set off once again from Woodstock, with me thinking, 'I'll be pleased to get back home.'

The first thing we did was to find the nearest garage - this thirsty camper wanted yet more petrol. Now we were on our way... accompanied by rain!

I'm the navigator, (hilarious, I'm useless reading a map); the first roundabout I shouted to John, 'First left!'... and he blithely carried on and we headed for miles along the wrong road before we found another roundabout to head back to the roundabout where John had gone wrong. By this time, he shouted at me for not shouting quickly enough, to which I replied, 'That's right, blame me, it's always my fault!' This was going to be a fun journey, I thought! Eventually we found our way to the M1 and were now heading in the right direction for home.

Someone once suggested that we get a Sat Nav! 'If John won't take notice of me he certainly wouldn't take notice of a box with a squeaky voice,' I replied.

It was a very quiet journey home from then onwards… John concentrating on driving and me thinking, 'Why does John blame me for everything going wrong?' By now I was in a black mood.

Eventually after approx. three long hours on the motorway, we pulled onto our driveway. The traffic had been heavy on the last two junctions of the M1. John had to concentrate and for some reason I'd had a job keeping awake. A cup of tea was called for before we even unloaded the camper. I was beginning to think, 'Have we done the right thing buying this camper? Was it ever going to work?' Only time would tell!

Somehow I had to get it over to John that I wasn't happy camping. Sleeping wasn't comfortable and there were several things I didn't like about it. I felt almost guilty about the whole thing, because John had always been keen on camping. (More so than I had.) I'd endured several holidays in the past with our touring caravan, not finding the pleasure that John appeared to find. Oh dear… trouble at mill.

This is where compromise, tolerance and coping come into the equation… not easy! We talked things over reasonably well and decided to give it another go, but on a campsite nearer to home next time.

We decided to give it another go after a couple of weeks

had gone by. Once again we loaded up the camper, edging slowly and carefully off our drive and headed for Worksop, the site being on National Trust land... Clumber Park, to be exact.

We signed in, paid our nightly fee and drove round to our allotted pitch. We made a cup of tea and sandwiches, then sat back and watched the other campers. There were far more caravans than campervans, plenty of activity all around. (We ourselves used to do all this when we had a caravan.) Levelling up, fetching water, sorting out kids with their bikes, waste water container placed underneath, hitch lock for safety, cool boxes with food being lifted out of the boot of the car, BBQ's... oh dear, the stuff they bring camping these days. Anyway, it kept us amused for some while watching all this activity.

We could see, now, why campervans seemed to be a favourite with the older generation. It was a lovely evening and we strolled round to the pay phone, BECAUSE... mobile phones didn't work on this site. There was wi-fi etc., but no mobile phone facility. John said there were too many trees to pick up a signal. This site was in acres of ground, surrounded by woodland and trees. To let our daughter know we were on site, I used the phone on site, costing 60p for twenty minutes. As the answer phone was all I could talk to... it cost me 60p for about 2 minutes. (No refund facility.) I ask you, have you ever tried talking for twenty minutes to an answer phone? I wasn't very pleased!

The sun began to sink behind the tall trees and

woodland, like a great red ball of fire. Many of the campers were now heading for the toilet block and showers, towels and wash bags in their arms. Kids, some in their jim-jams trotting back all clean and ready for bed. John and I followed suit a little later. Now it was time for sorting out the bed. I was praying for a better night's sleep this time. However, it turned out to be another uncomfortable night of clambering over each other for the nightly visits to the loo! (Another joy of being older, one has to visit the loo at night frequently.)

The next morning, the birds were chirping happily away... I was far from happy. I'm thinking now, 'This isn't going to work.' More trouble at mill!

We packed everything away and made for home - thankfully it wasn't far. I was quiet on the way back, unusual for me... John sensed something was wrong.

Again, we unloaded the camper, with me thinking, 'How the hell do I tell John? Because that's it, I've had enough... and I'm not going anywhere again in that blessed camper!' I had to calm down or there'd be an almighty row, something I didn't want.

A good friend of mine had told me that since Jack, her husband, had retired they'd had more arguments than in all their married life! Now I knew what she meant, and she had my sympathy. I never thought for one minute that John and I would disagree like we seemed to be doing lately.

Eventually John and I sat down to discuss what we were

going to do with the campervan. Much as I knew he wouldn't want what I was about to suggest, I had to be honest, and told him: 'I want to sell it.'

'We'll lose money over it,' he replied.

'I know that,' I said, 'but we made a mistake and mistakes cost money.'

We contacted a dealer and sold it, and YES, we made a loss... but the relief I felt was worth it. Now, it was back to the drawing board with John still wanting a campervan. We both knew that the layout was completely wrong for us last time... the search for what we wanted was not easy. But nothing in life is easy.

The two main things we were looking for was: (a) A toilet, and (b) the bed had to make up as two singles with a space in the centre for the nightly visits to the loo. (No more clambering over each other!) We made a list of requirements and set about finding a model to suit our list.

John was like a dog with a bone; he wouldn't give up on his dream of having another campervan, although our first one was soo wrong for us. This, in turn, drove me mad at times: that little voice inside my head night and day wouldn't shut up.

Months later, we just happened to be in the right place at the right time. We'd seen a camper we thought might suit us, but when we saw it, it was far too large for our driveway... and too large for John to handle. While I sat in the car waiting for John to walk around the compound, he came back excitedly and said, 'Just come and have a look at this one and see what you think!'

I hauled myself out of the car thinking, 'I expect this is a waste of time.' To my surprise though, I got inside and it ticked most of the boxes. John came back over to the car with me and we sat and talked it over. We both agreed that it had most of our requirements… but the price was a little more than we would like it to be. I suggested that John found a Salesman, to find out more about this camper. It was in very good condition and we didn't think it would stand around for long. If we really wanted it, we needed to act quickly and make a decision.

Apparently it had arrived in the compound just three hours earlier… a bereavement sale. Although it was ten years old, it only had 50,000 miles on the clock; it was a 2.0, diesel engine… so would be more economical to run than the petrol engine in our other camper van. After a haggle with the manager, the price suited our budget and we decided to take the plunge and buy it. (Although it was November.) No way would it still be there at the end of the winter. Now you can see why I remarked that we were in the right place at the right time.

Sometimes, one has to take a chance and compromise… I only hoped that I'd done the right thing in agreeing to us having another camper.

This time, I made it clear that we were going to do some short distances and get acquainted with everything before we set off on an overnight journey. I'd learned from our previous mistake and to take one step at a time. I wanted this venture to work and not end up another disaster. We simply couldn't afford to keep making mistakes.

Through the long dreary winter months, we started up the camper approximately every couple of weeks and went shopping in it. We didn't have a bad winter as such, just a cold and damp one. Certainly not the kind of weather to want to go and sit reading, or seeing the countryside.

However, March turned out to be very warm, almost like summer. In fact, I donned a summer dress on a couple of lovely days, saying to John, 'I hope this isn't our summer!' Many a true word spoken in jest, they tell us... for April was the coldest, wettest for decades. Oh dear, maybe I shouldn't have said what I did!

The few outings we enjoyed back in March were just a short distance away at Clumber Park. It was so warm we sat outside the camper in our folding chairs enjoying the sunshine... admiring the swans gliding on the beautiful lake, hearing the constant pecking of the woodpeckers, watching squirrels scurrying upwards, swinging from branch to branch through the trees with our binoculars. We sat talking to complete strangers, some locals, others on holiday breaks. One couple offered to take a photo of John and me together... quite a rare treat, and it turned out to be a lovely photo of us. This is what retirement should be like!

It's not all about days out though, the chores at home

still had to be done... shopping for food, mowing the grass (John's domain), then grabbing a few hours away in the camper whenever the weather obliged. One day we'll do an overnight stay somewhere not too far away for starters. We learned from our other campervan, not to try and run before we could walk... in other words, 'take one step at a time' (or, have half a pint and go steady... an old saying of John's granddad).

Secretly though, I wish I could get enthusiastic about camping like John does, it would make life easier. The older I get I like my home comforts more, and no one can say that any form of camping is 100% comfortable. Maybe it's the little boy inside John, who still sees camping as fun... after all, he was in the boy scouts for years.

Try not to be envious of the retired, who've worked hard throughout their lives... I've already mentioned that it's not all honey, and 'the grass isn't always greener.' There are many ups and downs even in retirement, just as there are in life itself.

Retirement takes a lot of adjusting. 24/7 can be quite hard at times. John and I have sampled 14 years now. How many more years we have is in the lap of the gods! Many more, I hope!

*   *   *

Like I said at the very beginning of this story, 'The grass

isn't always greener.' Retirement isn't always easy, it presents problems and you must learn how to cope, how to deal with them.

Growing old is like an old car... with parts wearing out. The older you become, the more hospital appointment dates appear on your calendar. Even the doctor's waiting room becomes a second home. The receptionist greets you as an old friend. Considering the fact that I have an abject fear of doctors, dentists and hospitals... this is not my idea of fun!

I find all this very difficult to cope with. Without John's support I don't know if I would even try to cope.

When one reaches the final stage of life, (in other words 'Retirement'), there are so many memories to look back upon, fewer moments to look forward to. However, the good times remain locked in the mind... there to be taken out and enjoyed, re-lived all over again at one's leisure.

Re-living the good times, fond memories of friends who entered our life... if only for a short period. Some friends we've lost, friends we've loved greatly, and this can hurt. (As with my friendship with Joan that ended after 60 years.)

Death of loved ones, bereavement, we sit in solace remembering those taken from us, to higher places. We have to let go and move forward. We don't forget, just learn to cope. Friends are precious, much more so in old age. We all need someone in our life for 'no man is an island'... a well-known proverb!

Age brings compensations. All that rushing around, now

in the past, gives way to sitting quietly. Depth of thinking is great. Time to listen to others' problems, wisdom to help and advise. Your experience may help others... After all, you've been there, done that, etc.

Everything in life, there's a reason for, even if we can't see that straight away!

Although John drives me to distraction at times, I sometimes think one gets to a crossroads in life where one can't live with someone... yet can't visualise life without them.

For instance... I cannot do a lot of the chores I used to do and find this very frustrating. I need space. I need to be left alone in (what was) MY KITCHEN and feel like shouting, 'Get out of my blessed kitchen!' But I keep these thoughts to myself. (For the sake of peace.)

It's lucky sometimes that other people cannot see inside the mind, especially when shopping at the supermarket, for instance. Being ignored at the checkout while the operator sits chatting to her colleague, totally ignoring the customer! My thought when this occurs: 'Am I invisible?' Also, someone's child misbehaving, throwing a tantrum, lying in the aisle and screaming, and I'm thinking, 'How do today's mothers tolerate this kind of behaviour, which they appear oblivious to?' I ask myself again and again, 'Why does she think I should love her badly behaved little treasure?' While I silently think, 'That treasure of a child could really do with a quick smack on her butt!' But nowadays parents mustn't be seen to chastise their child for fear of being reported to someone in high authority! When one studies the behaviour of children... a baby is born, a blank canvas... one has to acknowledge it's not born with evil intentions, bad manners, or naughty behaviour. It's up to the parents to cultivate their baby into a loving, well-mannered human being who shows respect for others. They need discipline, and examples of just how to achieve these traits. Just like a puppy needs to be trained, so does the baby. So many parents think it's the duty of the school, not only to educate their children, but to teach them moral values. This is wrong, parents have a duty to their children... and this begins at home!

I hope you can see from these examples how to cope with these situations... by keeping 'quiet', perhaps? At least it's my way of coping.

WHY?

Why did my father open the door that night? Whoever it was might just as well have shot him, for he just collapsed on the floor dying of a heart attack.

The elderly are vulnerable. NEVER open the door to anyone you don't know after dark.

If Dad hadn't been so trustworthy of everyone he might still be alive today!

*   *   *

My name is Sophie. I live approx. five miles away from my father, who is now in his late seventies. He's always been my friend as well as a good father.

Since my mother died around a year ago now, Dad's been living alone... fending for himself. Jim, my husband, and I visit him as often as time allows, at least once a week. But Dad's spending too many lonely hours, thinking. He has a carer, a sweet little woman, Maggie, who comes in daily, and also a good neighbour who shops for him. Jim and I, as well as Maggie his carer, all share in shopping for him.

Dad was recently diagnosed with type 2 diabetes. A bit

of a shock as he had no family history of diabetes. Connected with the diabetes and sugar levels, etc., he now needs extra medication, plus eye drops for the Glaucoma discovered when he attended his diabetes review.

Dad is very trusting. He has to be because of all the help he relies on to keep him going. I sat in their kitchen one night talking to him while Jim cut the grass for him. He told me, 'It's so bl**dy lonely being on your own, Sophie.'

As I remarked earlier, the elderly are very vulnerable. Villains, youngsters with vile intentions, prey on this. Because of this, Jim and I persuaded Dad to have a security device... something he can wear with a panic button to press if he needs help. It's a good thing we talked Dad into having this.

Dad's bungalow is situated on a main road with passing traffic and people scurrying by.

What happened to Dad occurred one dark winter's night. He sat watching a football match on TV while Mr Tibbs (as he was named) lay sprawled out in front of the fire... purring with contentment. Suddenly the doorbell rang! Not content with just ringing the bell and waiting, whoever it was, began hammering loudly on the door.

Now, Dad couldn't move quickly at his age. He wasn't used to visitors late at night either. So, with caution, he drew back the faded curtain and peered through the gloom. He didn't recognise whoever it was standing there. 'What do you want?' he growled. ('I must get a light fixed at the front door,' he thought.)

Dad was none too pleased at being disturbed in the middle of Chelsea's game against Everton. He'd been a keen follower of Chelsea in his younger days. Both he and a friend supported Chelsea and regularly went to watch when Chelsea played at home.

A voice answered Dad back: 'Sorry to disturb you Pop, but I think I've twisted or broken my ankle. Have you got a phone I could use to get me some help to the nearest A&E?'

Cross as he felt, Dad foolishly let the youth in, thinking he couldn't leave him to hobble any further.

I said at the beginning of this story that Dad was trusting. Too much so for his own good.

Once inside the youth slammed the door shut and turned on Dad, saying. 'Where d'yer keep yer cash Pop?' He roughly grabbed Dad, pinning him against the wall, threatening him by saying, 'Tell me and you'll come to no harm!'

'I can't breathe,' Dad gasped!

'Don't give me that crap!' the youth shouted. 'If you know what's good for you, give me what I want and I'll be gone. You won't ever see me again.'

With that, Dad threw a tin box at the youth, saying, 'That's all I've got, now clear off and leave me in peace!'

The youth grabbed the tin box and snatched the wallet from Dad's back pocket before running away... muttering a string of expletives as he sloped off into the gloom without a backward glance!

Panic, fear, rushed through my poor old dad as he slumped to the floor, clutching his pain racked chest.

Before Dad drifted into unconsciousness, he pressed the panic button. A little later when I got to him, I found him lying in the hallway. I cradled his head while he told me what had happened. His breathing was very shallow and his words almost a whisper as his story unfolded. I kept saying to him, 'Don't talk Dad' - but he insisted on me knowing the events and he wouldn't give up.

'Sophie,' he whispered, 'promise me you'll see that he's found and bring justice to bear on him... promise me, then I'll die happy!'

'You're not going to die, Dad, you mustn't!' I cried, 'What would I do without you?'

With that he breathed his last breath and passed away in my arms. My only consolation is this... I was with him, so he didn't die alone.

I called the ambulance, then called the police. But by then Dad was dead - there was nothing anyone could do.

If only he hadn't opened his door that night, he might still be alive. I've written this story to prove just how vulnerable the elderly are.

THOMAS

Is there anything other than this life as we know it on earth? What happens when we die? That's a well-kept secret, except for my friend Thomas, who is a great believer in the resurrection, the afterlife!

*　　*　　*

I have this friend who I shall name Thomas. For obvious reasons I won't use his real name. My name is Sally, but really it should be Thomas - for I'm so different from my friend Thomas! I am more the 'doubting Thomas' in the Holy Bible. I always need proof of whatever I am told, or led to believe.

Now, my friend Thomas is so different, in as much as he's a real believer in the resurrection. This is proof that opposites attract.

Because Thomas is so different to me, I admire him. I'm attracted to him for many reasons. He's outgoing, charming, yet sincere. He sees good in everyone, yet like myself... he falls by the wayside sometimes. He admits to struggling with keeping the Ten Commandments at times, especially number five, 'Thou shalt not commit adultery.' This proves to me that Thomas is human. Just like myself.

Anyone can commit adultery in the mind, without any physical contact... just by means of the imagination. It's good to have a sincere friendship, like mine is with Thomas. We trust each other implicitly, knowing that whatever we confide to each other is just that - confidential, not to be repeated!

We share a liking for the same kind of music. I love our friendship and would be devastated if it ended or were destroyed.

I'm very fond of Thomas as the brother that I never had the joy of sharing my life with. Thomas suffers bouts of depression, as do I at times. Because of this I understand just how he feels when he can't see the light at the end of the tunnel. I empathize with this entirely. Maybe that's why Thomas confides in me. Because he confides in me, I see the REAL Thomas, warts and all, as people say!

Others see what Thomas allows them to see, and no more. We are opposites in many ways. He's more intellectual than me. He's my cultured friend. He compliments me often in so many ways, which I admit to enjoying. He admires my creativity and energy. We may be like 'chalk and cheese', but we go together and complement each other. What a perfect combination we make!

Thomas is a loner. He gets restless when faced with mundane chores. However, he's a man who loves to travel. His devout faith will see him through any crisis. How I wish I could say the same about myself!

This is why I said previously at the very beginning, *my* name should have been Thomas... for I always doubt myself... afraid, and it's this fear that holds me back. It always has!

If only I could be more like my friend Thomas, and accept things. Instead of which, I fight my way through situations. Then I get stressed and depressed.

Thomas sees a house as an investment. I see it as a home... two very different aspects of a property. This is strange really because Thomas is a big family man. But then, Thomas is a businessman. I am a wife and mother - grandmother too: maybe this has something to do with why we're so different with our ideas! Yet, Thomas is also a grandfather, and a great grandfather too.

A touch of envy, as expressed by the Commandment, 'Thou shalt not covet thy neighbour's wife...' is there too. It's not really avarice or greed on Thomas's part. Just another of his human traits. We're all guilty of this sometimes.

Sometimes Thomas envies my state of mind when I say, quite truthfully, 'I have something money can't buy, peace and contentment of mind.'

Thomas lives life on a ' cliff edge' - he craves excitement, fulfilment. Don't we all crave this sometimes? With Thomas though, he thrives on this.

Thomas loves his tipple, scotch or a 'wee dram' as he calls it. I am tea total, for no apparent reason - I just don't care much for drink... other than tea or coffee. Another of our differences. Nothing of importance, just a matter of different tastes.

Thomas can be impulsive and plunges in, (hang the consequences), whereas I am cautious. I really pray that our friendship will last for many more years.

I would be sad if it turned out to be a 'brief encounter friendship.'

Thoughts

Carried along on the wind,
are my thoughts of you.
Driven silently in my mind,
I earnestly pray for you.

Mundane tasks I perform, as you do,
while I quietly think of you.
Thoughts driven in the wind I send -
especially for you, my treasured friend!

God bless.

There is a vast difference between a friend and an acquaintance. Many friends enter our lives for a brief period, whilst others become lifetime friends. Some people claim to have a great number of friends, (my own daughter being one of them), BUT, a REAL friend is that special someone to share confidences with. These friends are often whittled down to a mere handful!

Count yourself lucky to enjoy just that handful I mention in the latter group, that small remnant of special friends.

Amen.

THE HAUNTED HOUSE

'This is spooky!' said George as we trudged along the woodland towards the Old Manor House!

'Hold my hand then, you big girl's blouse!' I answered.

By now it was raining stair rods, our flimsy T-shirts clinging to our bodies like limpets. Suddenly the sky lit with a zigzag flash of lightening, followed by a tremendous bang. George gripped my hand even tighter with his sweaty palms.

'Do you think this is a good idea?' he asked.

'Would you rather we turned back?' I said. 'NO, George, you know why we're here, we must see it through now we've got this far!'

Dave, the editor of the newspaper we worked for, stressed that whoever came up with a front-page story would be well rewarded.

Feeling very shaken, I said to George, 'Look over there!' I felt sick with fear at the sight of a leg protruding from out of the ground.

'Oh my God!' exclaimed George, 'Let's get out of here!'

'No way George, this is the kind of discovery to make front page news!' I said, steadying my nerves. 'The very reason we're here. Where's your mobile phone?'

He searched his pockets... no phone!

'Lucky you've got me!' I shrieked at him hysterically. I dialled for the police, who asked where we were. That was hard to answer.

After what seemed a long time we spotted car headlights beaming through the bare trees. The police had arrived and began to cordon off the area.

Some while later and the police walked towards where George and I were waiting, carrying an artificial limb in their hand. Did we feel stupid, calling the police out!

'Will we be charged with wasting police time?' I asked tentatively.

'Not on this occasion, Annabel,' the officer proclaimed. 'But, please tell us precisely what you were doing here in the grounds of the haunted Manor House?'

They quite understood when we explained we were journalists for a national newspaper, trying to make front-page news. Without further ado they bade us goodnight and went on their way!

We were on our own again. We began slowly walking in the direction of the old Manor House. With the amount of rain that had recently fallen, what had been a beautiful lake was now a very flooded and overflowing stream.

The silhouette of a gondola, with a woman dressed in grey, drifted silently along, before disappearing into the misty gloom. Before it completely disappeared... a noise that sounded like a stifled sobbing rang out. It was weird!

Even a tawny owl perched high in the bare trees added to the mysticism of this place... as it hooted out loud!

George said, 'Come on Annabel, let's get the hell out of here!'

We turned around and fled back the way we'd come... with hearts pounding. We collapsed on the ground and got our breath back eventually.

'I wonder if that's why it's called the haunted house?' said George

'Maybe,' I replied.

Suddenly George went down on one knee. Looking up into my eyes, he said, 'I've always fancied you Annabel, will you marry me?'

'Of course I will,' I replied. 'What took you so long to ask me?'

Well, George and I did make front-page news! Not quite the way we'd expected, BUT, it was headlines just the same:

'George Banks, our senior journalist, proposed to Annabel Roberts in the grounds of the nearby haunted Manor House... they will become man and wife later this year.'

The end...?

A PLEASANT DAY OUT...
OR WAS IT?

Whatever happened to the Highway Code, the way I was taught to drive? It seems that it no longer exists. Common courtesy to others, good manners... For instance, 'Do not park across someone's driveway?' Acknowledging a driver for waiting to let you through. All this seems to be a thing of the past nowadays. Common sense also appears to be missing.

How are today's drivers being taught? The way I see it, 'Every man for himself seems to be the new Highway Code!' (Or, 'I'm all right Jack!')

I'm feeling somewhat aggrieved after our day out yesterday, which was spoilt by other inconsiderate drivers. I'm talking here about 'tailgating'! In other words, driving dangerously near to the boot of the car in front. This makes both my husband and myself (the passenger), stressed to say the least!

I have a friend who admits, when this happens to him... he does one of two movements. He either turns left at the first road he can, or he pulls into a lay-by, hoping the tailgater will pass him. He also drives slowly, hoping the offender will pass him... but often that doesn't work.

Because this happens frequently, tailgating, I mean, he feels obliged to drive faster than he's happy with. (Sometimes this amounts to driving over the official speed limit for the area.) Who will pay the fine if he's caught on camera? Him, of course. Not only a fine, but points on his driving licence. And what do points mean? Too many points, no driving licence! When he does shake off the offender, his heart is beating 100 beats to the minute... and he's now stressed as well as angry. (This doesn't do his BP much good either.)

My husband and I, as well as my friend, are in our seventies! You might think, like so many younger drivers do, that we should no longer be driving on today's roads. Because of our age, we're unsafe! BUT, here's the question to ask: why is it then, that the older driver is offered much lower car insurance than the younger one? Because he's a safer driver is the answer! He's also more experienced, and more cautious.

I know of three young drivers living nearby who, having passed their driving test at the first attempt, all had accidents within the first six months of being on the road! One of them completely overturned his car outside the Royal Hospital in Derbyshire where I live. Obviously he lost control of his car. (I did think to myself, 'Well, at least he was near to the A&E Department!') There was no other vehicle involved - he just hadn't got enough experience to know his car and his own capabilities.

Many drivers, whether they are young or elderly, do not drive according to the weather. Just because they normally get to their destination or place of work in a certain time, it doesn't mean that it can still be done on a 'foggy morning' or driving through a torrential downpour, even a snowstorm. Slow down, be sensible. NO, that would be asking too much of today's drivers it seems!

I found many years ago that you REALLY start to learn to drive AFTER you pass your test. The reason being, for the first time you have to think for yourself... plan your route, etc., with no one sitting beside you saying, 'Turn right/left at the next junction.'

Back to our day out yesterday, we both ended up stressed to say the least. We had a driver tailgating us for miles through the Chatsworth Estate. We approached a roundabout where we signalled right towards Chesterfield and our tailgater then drew alongside me (the passenger) and we both thought 'thank goodness, he's going to Stockport/Manchester' (as signposted), but NO, he suddenly swerved right in front of us and cut us up completely! Neither of us could believe what he'd done! We've had many drivers overtake us on the right-hand side on a roundabout... but NEVER on the left! Is this another new option in today's Highway Code? Maybe I should buy a copy of the new Highway Code and study it closely!

What is it about today's drivers that make them drive like a 'bat out of hell', at breakneck speed? Do they really want to arrive early in the next world so much?

Each time we venture forth in our car or campervan, I'm feeling apprehensive. What should be a pleasurable day out, enjoying the beautiful countryside, is often spoilt by these maniacs who call themselves drivers. They not only risk their own lives with their dangerous, reckless driving... BUT others as well. They are selfish, thinking only of themselves and how quickly they can get from A to B in the shortest time. They probably end up in their local at night, boasting about how quickly they got to their destinations that very day.

While they're about it, they most likely boast about how they'd overtaken some 'old fool' who was only driving at around 50 miles per hour... and how they'd put their foot down and sped past at lightning speed. (Omitting to say anything about the motorist coming in the opposite direction, who'd flashed his lights at him.)

I dislike roundabouts, especially when I see a foreign lorry speeding towards MY side (the passenger side) of the car. On the Continent those already on the roundabout are supposed to give way to vehicles approaching... whereas here in England we give way to those already on the roundabout. If they drive in our Country, they should abide by our Highway Code. (If in Rome, do as the Romans do, especially when driving.)

I can understand why we hear of so many overturned lorries; they don't slow down enough when approaching from the slip-road, BUT virtually SWING on. One cannot always move over to the fast lane because of traffic from behind racing at full throttle. Hence, the lorry jams on his brakes too late to avoid a collision, most often ending up overturned across all three lanes, straight into the crash barrier.

Not only are lorries guilty of accidents on roundabouts, but motorists who dive in, in front of vehicles and get away with it, sometimes with seconds to spare. Is it any wonder we hear of so many accidents on roundabouts? They may get away with this reckless driving 99.9% of the time, but there's always that 0.1% chance of an accident.

Throughout Derbyshire the councils have erected signs EVERYWHERE it seems that say, 'Think Bike'… I know what *I* think of bikers! They dive in and out of lines of motorists, zigzagging as they go. Who comes off worst if they don't make it back in time? They do, of course. Does it deter them from this dangerous practice? NO, it doesn't! At what cost to the ratepayer have these signs been erected? I feel like suggesting that a new sign should be designed for the benefit of bikers… something like 'Think car'… but would that solve anything? I think not.

Have you ever been to Matlock Bath on a Sunday afternoon? If not, you've missed seeing hundreds of bikers gathering together. It's mayhem trying to get through these bikers as they congregate. Since living here in the Derbyshire Dales, we've learnt not to venture out at weekends or Bank holidays… so we're imprisoned in our own home.

After travelling many miles on today's roads, we hear of bad accidents and other innocent drivers held up for hours due to selfish actions from motorists. Is it any wonder there are so many accidents on today's roads? Personally I'm surprised there aren't more accidents!

Hey-ho, where shall we go tomorrow... How many of my nine lives have I got left? I feel like a cat with nine lives very often. Today's roads are no picnic, whether you're the driver or the passenger!

I used to drive regularly... BUT nowadays I have no wish to get behind the wheel. In fact, when I see my husband driving at fifty miles per hour, and other drivers pass him like a bat out of hell... I know for definite they would be passing me going gently along at 40-45 miles per hour.

So keep death off the roads is my motto... I'll remain a passenger.

POETRY

PAUSE FOR A WHILE

We are what we are.
We are who we are.
We can try to change,
however,
whatever
is within
stays forever.

We cannot change the past,
just hope for a better future.

Good intentions are the food of life.
Whatever we do,
or choose to do,
love and warmth will shine through
from within.

Each one of us is unique.
Some have a stubborn streak.
It's no surprise
we often disguise
true feelings.
Our nearest and dearest
see through this camouflage we display.
Seeing through our hopes and fears,
drying our tears,
in the living years!

Love and kindness penetrate

the heart
of the receiver.
Shut the gate
to those
feelings of jealousy and hate
from others.
Jealousy is like that of a poisonous snake
whose venom can kill.

Envy has no charm,
it can only harm
those it attacks!

Leave all these thoughts behind.
Climb aboard the bus of happiness
alongside me.
We'll travel it together!

DEMENTIA

Where has she gone?
Lost in her own world,
cut off from civilization,
and her family,
so unrecognisable!
Eyes that shone with love
in youth,
shone with health -
now vacant and staring.
Lifeless fingers, gnarled with age
that were once busy.
Green fingers that tended plants.
Fingers that sewed laboriously,
knitted, painted,
now lie still and lifeless in her lap!
Worthless, useless and agitated,
frustrated,
encapsulated
in a time zone,
alone!
To her family, she's gone!
They can only look on
with aching hearts,
knowing she'll never return
as the mother they knew.
This sad person
is the mother they knew and love.
Dementia is cruel,
it's a mental illness.
The mental anguish,

lives within the minds of the onlookers.
They can only watch their loved one
fade into oblivion.
This cruel disease has stolen her away to another world!

ETERNAL FRIENDSHIP

The crack in your heart,
the doubt in your faith,
I share with you.

Your sadness reflects
like a moonbeam
as it bounces
into my life!

I share,
because I care.
Your hurt
becomes my hurt.
Your sadness,
becomes my sadness,
because I care.
I'll always be there
for you
my treasured friend.

I'll share your grief
and your sorrow.
I'll be here,
today, always, tomorrow.
Just let me into your heart
and thoughts...

BULLYING TACTICS

Bullying often begins at school.
The perpetrator thinks it's cool!
The victim keeps quiet... fear rules here.

Bullying happens with drivers today,
white vans, lorries, the family car gives way!
For fear of repercussion... road rage!

Road rage, a common occurrence every day.
Yet more bullying and it's here to stay!
Fear of reprisal, we struggle to remain calm!

Conversation, interruptions... bullying tactics, the modern way.
Shouting us down, what can we say?
Not a lot, the bully says it all.

The elderly often spoken to in a patronising way.
Too vulnerable to complain, it happens every day.
These BULLIES are very often CARERS!

FATAL ATTRACTION

You're such a cracker.
Give me a smacker!
You know you want to....

Am I your cracker?
I'll give you a smacker,
because I want to...

Just think I'll mention,
I crave attention,
just like you do...

JEALOUSY

Jealousy is a poisonous snake!
How much more of your poisonous venom
can I take?

There's no love in jealousy,
only hate.
Your jealousy turned MY love
to hate!
At any rate,
that's how I see it.

What have I got
that you want so much?
I can't bear to feel your touch
any more,
that's for sure!

What have I got
that you want so much?
Whatever it may be,
don't envy me!

ABSENCE

Your absence broke my heart.
I hated us being apart.
Let me make it very plain.
I want you back again.

Your absence breaks my heart.
I hate it so much when we're apart.
Your absence gives me so much pain.
Please come back to me again.

You set my heart afire.
Filling it with strong desire.
Too much absence, CAN make the heart grow stronger.
Too much absence, CAN make it wonder?

Your absence really breaks my heart.
I really hate us being apart.
I'm nothing on my own.
It's like hell on earth, here alone.

Please hear my silent plea,
and hurry back home to me...

HUNGER

Are you hungry?
What are you hungry for,
food, possessions?
I am hungry.
Hungry for love,
sincerity, friendship!
Send me your love
to quench my appetite,
make my world right!
Whatever you hunger for,
share your thoughts with me,
you'll then see
it will lift your heart and mine!
I want to see your eyes shine.
Shine into mine.
That glance of admiration
fills my heart with joy.
Sensations tingle through me.
Dreams become reality.
Feelings like this are priceless!
Come to me!
I sense you're hurting deep inside,
don't let manly pride
keep you at a distance.
Love for a friend,
will help to mend
and soothe your troubled mind!
Let me paint your grey sky
BLUE again and
brush those clouds away.

A hug, a kiss,
wouldn't go amiss!
Take my hand,
let me guide you to happiness.
Just come to me...

PICTURED IN MY MIND

Deep in the depths of winter,
I walked in the freezing rain.
Dressed beyond recognition,
rain turned to snow again!

Trudging along through woodland,
footprints imprinted the snow,
fluffy white boughs of the trees,
crystallized at night, they glow!

An owl hooted, perched high on a branch,
snow glistening white, what a chance,
my camera can't capture this magnificence,
it was lost in the deep winter snow.

With no camera to capture this wonderland,
it's imprinted in my brain,
like something one cannot describe,
branches hanging wet with snow, now turned to rain.

YOU'LL ALWAYS REMAIN
IN MY HEART

Unrequited love pierces the heart
like an arrow.
Pain so sharp, like a dart.
Grief lingers on, painful though it be
the one you grieve, you no longer see.
Only in mind
solace can you find.

Just as Robbie Burns once said:
A symbol of love, the rose, so red...

THE KISS

First, imagination -
then, anticipation.
Feelings of being locked in your arms;
That embrace,
I stroke your face
prior to lips locking together.
Your lips meet mine -
a tingling sensation surges throughout.
Do you feel it too?
Are you, like me,
on another planet?
All this emotion,
bursts forth in the explosion
as our lips entwine,
yours and mine.
This kiss has the element,
the ingredient,
for love!
Love can build bridges.
We don't need bridges,
our kiss is overflowing with love!

WRONG TIME...WRONG PLACE

The moment we met,
our eyes said it all.
How could I ever forget,
just how easy it is to fall...
IN LOVE!

Wrong time,
wrong place,
how could I ever forget your face?

I was born years too soon.
In the wrong place.
Timing was so wrong.
You were born too late!

Wrong time,
wrong place,
how could I ever forget your face?

Life and age was wrong it seemed.
But you'll remain a part of my life.
You were perfect, just as I'd dreamed.

Wrong time,
wrong place,
how could I ever forget your face?

THINK ABOUT IT

There are no pockets in a shroud.
We enter this world with nothing,
and we leave with nothing!

The more possessions we accumulate,
the more we leave behind
at our demise!

Whether you be rich or poor,
for sure,
when the final curtain falls,
all that remains,
are memories,
whether they are good or bad,
happy or sad!

Friendship can mean so much.
A tender touch.
Collect friends,
they're more precious
than possessions!
Just like an antique,
friends become more valuable with time.

BYGONE TIMES

Thrills, feelings, sensations!
All these are living proof
of excitement.
Can't you just feel it?
If not feel it,
imagine it!
That tingling sensation
you feel with first love,
full of passion.
Was it really love,
or was it lust?
Whatever...
it was soo pleasurable.
Those memorable kisses,
Those hugs,
Those searches,
That finding out
about each other!
Finding out what pleased,
(or what teased).
Was it really so many years ago?
Why, when did this body
age so much
that only memories remain?
How I'd love to do it all again.
BUT, true love never dies,
it remains in the heart forever.
While the heart beats
and eyes meet....
love can flourish once more,
that's for sure.

PER-CHANCE... LOVER

The first time we came face to face.
The first time I felt the warmth of your embrace.
I wonder if you felt it too,
that feeling I felt for you?
You stole my heart.
And since that day we've been apart.
Can love be born in such a short while?
You captivated me with your smile.
I feel your presence every day,
likening you to a ' summer's day' -
full of warmth, compassion, strength and love.
Your body towered over mine, from way above!
Please, never change, never falter,
whatever you do, try not to alter.
I savour your calm, cultured, sexy voice.
Capturing the moment, listening again, would be my choice!
Your aroma stored in a bottle, so divine,
not to be shared, entirely mine.
Fantasizing of you each day and night,
although this pleasure, I really have no right.
Per-chance, is all I can be allowed.
Imagination, sighting your face in a crowd.
Reality hits so hard, you're not there it seems.
My mind encapsulates your image in dreams!
Memories I've stored in mind forever.
Memories that are mine for ever and ever!
Just for me alone to treasure.
Depth of love, impossible to measure!

You could be my 'Romeo' - could I be your Juliet?
I'm not sure of the answer yet!

'Safely clasped in your embrace,
softly pressed against your face!'

*(For anyone who's experienced true,
pure, unadulterated love…)*

TOPS

You're my top man.
You're my top friend!
Best man.
Best friend!
Right to the bitter end,
these are what you are!

Top dog.
Top friend!
Right to the bitter end,
unconditional love you send!

I'm your constant friend.
My constant love I'll always send.
Right to the bitter end!

ANOTHER BIRTHDAY

Another year has flown away,
my hair is slowly turning grey!

Where did the blonde bombshell go,
that's what I want to know?

There's nothing different about today,
why should it be different anyway?

Because it's MY BIRTHDAY...

HISTORY

We are history,
living proof of life on earth.
History repeats,
weather patterns repeat
down the decades!
We've read about the ice-age,
Centuries ago, humans lived through the 'Ice-age'.
We now have 'Global warming'!
Generations will live through this experience,
just as our forebears did!
Volcanic eruptions.
Earthquakes.
Hurricanes.
Landslides.
Tsunami's.
Flooding.
All these catastrophes are happening!
We'll live through them and procreate.
This is life,
this is history in the making!
We are lucky to live in these times,
we are living history.
Future generations will read of this,
just as we read about the 'ice-age'.
This is the Twenty-First Century.
Things are moving forward at a faster pace,
BUT, how much faster can things continue to go?
Do you know?
The Twenty-First Century technology is awesome,
BUT, will mankind get too clever?

Nothing and no one lasts forever!
Will there be a Big Bang?
The Bible predicts many such happenings!
How long before time runs out,
that's the big question?
Will the ice cap melt and flood the earth again,
or will the sun burn everything on the earth
we know and love?
When will the Messiah return?

Footnote:
History was made by Neil Armstrong, the first man to step
on the moon. Sadly, today, the 25th Aug. 2012, he passed
away at the age of 82.

ARE YOU THERE?

Where were YOU, when I needed you?
Your silence was so cruel.
Where were YOU, when I needed you?
Your absence was so cruel.

Where were YOU, when I needed you?
I wanted just a little of your time.
Was that such a crime?
Do you still remember me?

I was once your friend...

BORROWED LOVE

You're akin to a drug,
a craving,
I cannot resist.
Like a drug,
I can't get you out of my system,
however hard I try.
WHY?
I sometimes wish we'd never met,
YET,
look what joy I'd have missed.
Along with joy,
you brought me sorrow.
I have to share you,
I can only borrow,
for you can never be mine
entirely.
You remarked,
we're stuck with each other!
That's not love,
you called HER cuddly once,
not any more though.
What happened, between then and now?
You shouted at her once in temper,
'You're a big fat cow'…
She retorted,
'You're a boring old f*rt!'
Is she the woman you fell in love with
so many years ago?
I don't think so!
If only

we could lie together,
and cuddle up close,
wrapped in each other's arms...
paradise would be here on earth.
For what it's worth,
I'd give the world to be in her shoes,
I'd never want to lose
your love!

ENCHANTED

Hold me close,
hold me tight,
dancing in the moonlight.

Let this waltz last forever.
Let this waltz blend us together.

I sense your beating heart...close to mine.
Let this moment last forever, it's so divine.
I feel your breath, mingled with mine.
Let the moonlight forever shine!

Ensconced in your arms,
bewitched with your charms,
nothing else I need...it calms!

Press your face even closer to mine,
let this moment in time stand still, two bodies entwine,
yours with mine....

I GIVE MY ALL

I have nothing
yet, I have everything.

I bring everything
to love and friendship
YET, I expect nothing
in return!

I give you trust.
This is a must
in any union!

I give everything
BUT, expect nothing.
THIS, avoids disappointment!

FOND MEMORIES

Memories live within forever
without fading.
Not like us humans,
who age.
Memories can be brought out,
relived again...giving yet more pleasure!
Memories are a treasure -
buried inside a treasure chest.
A chest, the owner has the key
to open!
Vivid memories of bygone days -
still clear and vibrant.
So much so, we relive the thrill
and excitement all over again.
Sensual fragrance wafts
through once again.
Tasting those luscious lips again!
The thrill of that first union,
togetherness,
intimacy,
unforgettable closeness!
Reliving that tingling sensation
before the explosion.
Memories no one can steal,
they are still so real,
although they're now just memories -
they're priceless!

MYSTICAL

I had a dream,
or so it would seem!
BUT, what was it?
A longing
for past pleasures,
moments to treasure,
memories, imagination -
playing tricks in my dream?
Bygone sensations,
that were lost in the past.
Fulfilment, happiness,
breathlessness!
When I awoke I was breathless,
realising it was just a dream!
Was it something spiritual?
It was divine,
I know that much.
There was no touch,
nothing physical,
but mystical.
And, it was all over too soon!
Was it a fantasy
of unknown love for someone?
I could reach
a climax,
without touch,
it proved that much.
Was it a dream,
as it would seem?
What do you think?

SAFE, SECURE

Tuck me under your wing.
Shelter me as in a sling.
Hold me close to your breast,
I need the safe haven of your chest!
Fill my heart with love and joy,
engulf my whole being, darling boy.
Worlds apart, yet you touch my soul,
worlds apart, yet you make me whole!
Fond thoughts and memories creep into mind -
BUT, where are you? Close the blind.
The pedestal I place you upon is so high,
it reaches up towards the sky.
All I need is to lie with you!
Caress you, whisper, dream with you.
Kiss those inviting lips.
Touch them gently with my fingertips.
Is this thinking in my head
when I want to climb into your bed?
You could be my world -
instead of my dream world.
Make a move, you know you want to,
just as much as I do...

FORGIVENESS IS THE KEY

Forgiveness is the key
to World Peace.
Trust, is a must!
It's never too late
to free your mind of
HATE!
Treat others the way
you like them to treat you.
Finally, never forget -
the 'Meek shall inherit the earth'…

I'M AT A LOSS

Your friendship meant a lot to me,
BUT, you couldn't see
that friendship is a two-way thing.

Where are you now?

You held my happiness
in your palm
of fragility
and you crushed me.
Still, you couldn't see
that friendship is a two-way affair!

SORRY

Is it really so difficult to say 'I'm sorry'?
Think about it before you answer, don't hurry.
Is it a fact that you can't own up to being wrong?
Did you want to apologise all along?
If you choke at the thought... send a letter,
that could be even better!
You're not perfect, neither am I,
say 'sorry', NOT 'goodbye'!
It seems you couldn't forgive and forget,
how I wish we'd never met.
It's taken me a long time to see
you didn't ever know the real me!
All those years of friendship lost,
and at such a huge cost.
Was it so difficult to say 'sorry'?
Not if you meant it, but not to worry.
I thought our friendship was really strong,
seems I was wrong.
In the end it's you who'll lose,
Next time I'll be careful who I choose
as a friend...

NEEDS

Everyone needs someone,
just as I need you,
you need me too!

Everyone needs someone,
just as I need you
when I'm feeling blue!

Everyone needs someone,
just as I need you
to share happy moments with - how true!

Everyone needs someone,
this is true,
even a loner, like you!

Everyone needs someone,
no one is an island,
NOT even YOU!

MARS

Why is mankind so interested in Mars?
Wanting to land a vehicle,
up there amongst the stars.
What is the attraction
of this planet
so many light years away from earth?
Whatever makes this venture worth
so many millions?
Millions of starving people,
millions of people in debt.
Why this obsession
when there's depression -
businesses going broke daily
here on planet earth?
Is it really worth
millions, billions, trillions,
with so much deprivation
everywhere!

This is the real world!
It's anyone's guess
how we'll get out of the mess
we humans have created...

FROM A DISTANCE

I wonder what you're doing,
when you're far away from me?

I wonder what you're thinking,
when you're far away from me?

I wonder who you're thinking of,
when you're far away from me?

Would it be presumptuous,
imagining your thoughts include me?

I often find, you in my mind,
when you're far away from me!

Imagination plays a part,
when you're far away from me.

Do you imagine togetherness,
when you're away from me?

Do you feel a closeness,
when you're far away from me?

Do you imagine that sensual aroma,
that flows from inside me?

I can sense all of these things,
although you're far away from me!

Because that's how it will always be -
distance between the two of us... you and me!

[This poem could be set to music!]

MAGICAL

There's a brilliant moon tonight,
and it's really shining bright,
a beacon of delight.
Don't you just love it?

There's a brilliant moon tonight,
the snow is sparkling white,
this is such a pure delight.
Don't you just love it?

There's a brilliant moon tonight,
Christmas time is a delight,
the weather is just right.
Don't you just love it?

There's a brilliant moon tonight,
don't you love this magic sight,
snowy weather's come just right.
Don't you just love it?
I know that I do…

[This poem could be set to music!]